THE FATHERS OF NEW ENGLAND

EXTRA-ILLUSTRATED EDITION

∵

VOLUME 6
THE CHRONICLES
OF AMERICA SERIES
ALLEN JOHNSON
EDITOR

GERHARD R. LOMER
CHARLES W. JEFFERYS
ASSISTANT EDITORS

THE FATHERS OF NEW ENGLAND

A CHRONICLE OF THE PURITAN COMMONWEALTHS
BY CHARLES M. ANDREWS

NEW HAVEN: YALE UNIVERSITY PRESS
TORONTO: GLASGOW, BROOK & CO.
LONDON: HUMPHREY MILFORD
OXFORD UNIVERSITY PRESS

CONTENTS

I. THE COMING OF THE PILGRIMS   Page   1

II. THE BAY COLONY   "   21

III. COMPLETING THE WORK OF SETTLEMENT   "   45

IV. EARLY NEW ENGLAND LIFE   "   72

V. AN ATTEMPT AT COLONIAL UNION   "   88

VI. WINNING THE CHARTERS   "   100

VII. MASSACHUSETTS DEFIANT   "   116

VIII. WARS WITH THE INDIANS   "   129

IX. THE BAY COLONY DISCIPLINED   "   147

X. THE ANDROS RÉGIME IN NEW ENGLAND   "   166

XI. THE END OF AN ERA   "   194

BIBLIOGRAPHICAL NOTE   "   201

INDEX   "   205

ILLUSTRATIONS

EDWARD WINSLOW

The only authentic portrait of a *Mayflower* Pilgrim. Painted in England in 1651, possibly by Walker, the well-known miniature painter. In the collection at Pilgrim Hall, Plymouth, Massachusetts.   *Frontispiece*

COLONIAL NEW ENGLAND, 1620–1690

Map by W. L. G. Joerg, American Geographical Society.   *Facing page*   16

JOHN WINTHROP

Painting by Charles Osgood, 1834, copied from the original in the State House, Boston. In the collection of the Massachusetts Historical Society, Boston.   "   "   *32*

SWORD OF MILES STANDISH, IRON POT AND PEWTER PLATTER, BROUGHT BY STANDISH IN THE *MAYFLOWER*

ELDER BREWSTER'S CHAIR, AND CRADLE OF PEREGRINE WHITE, THE FIRST PILGRIM BABY

In the collection at Pilgrim Hall, Plymouth, Massachusetts.   "   "   *48*

SAMUEL SEWALL, CHIEF JUSTICE OF MASSACHUSETTS

Copy of the original painting. In the collection of the Massachusetts Historical Society, Boston.   "   "   *64*

THE "WITCH HOUSE," SALEM, MASSACHU-
SETTS, IN WHICH LIVED JUDGE CORBIN,
AND WHEREIN SOME OF THE PRELIMI-
NARY EXAMINATIONS FOR WITCHCRAFT
WERE HELD. Photograph taken about 1855.
In the collection of the Essex Institute, Salem,
Massachusetts.

HOUSE BUILT IN 1684, SHOWING THE PRO-
JECTING UPPER STORY OF AN EARLY
NEW ENGLAND HOUSE. In the grounds
of the Essex Institute, Salem, Massachusetts. *Facing page 80*

SIMON BRADSTREET. Painting in the State
House, Boston.

JOHN ENDECOTT. Painting in the collection
of the Massachusetts Historical Society, Boston. "   "   96

JOSEPH DUDLEY. Painting in the collection of
the Massachusetts Historical Society, Boston.

SIR EDMUND ANDROS. Engraving from the
original painting owned by descendants of Andros
in London, England. Reproduced in *The Andros
Tracts*, published by the Prince Society, Boston. "   "   160

THE REVEREND COTTON MATHER, AGED 65
Engraving by P. Pelham, 1727, after his own
drawing from life. The first mezzotint engraving
made in America. Reproduced from a copy in
the collection of the Massachusetts Historical
Society, Boston. "   "   176

THE REVEREND INCREASE MATHER
Painting by Job Vanderspruyt, 1688. In the
collection of the Massachusetts Historical Society, Boston. "   "   192

THE FATHERS OF NEW ENGLAND

$\cdot\cdot\cdot$

CHAPTER I

THE COMING OF THE PILGRIMS

THE Pilgrims and Puritans, whose migration to the New World marks the beginning of permanent settlement in New England, were children of the same age as the enterprising and adventurous pioneers of England in Virginia, Bermuda, and the Caribbean. It was the age in which the foundations of the British Empire were being laid in the Western Continent. The " spacious times of great Elizabeth " had passed, but the new national spirit born of those times stirred within the English people. The Kingdom had enjoyed sixty years of domestic peace and prosperity, and Englishmen were eager to enter the lists for a share in the advantages which the New World offered to those who would venture therein. Both landowning and

1

landholding classes, gentry and tenant farmers
alike, were clamoring, the one for an increase of
their landed estates, the other for freedom from the
feudal restraints which still legally bound them.
The land-hunger of neither class could be satisfied
in a narrow island where the law and the lawgivers
were in favor of the maintenance of feudal rights.
The expectations of all were aroused by visions
of wealth from the El Dorados of the West, or of
profit from commercial enterprises which appealed
to the cupidity of capitalists and led to invest-
ments that promised speedy and ample returns.
A desire to improve social conditions and to
solve the problem of the poor and the vagrant,
which had become acute since the dissolution of the
monasteries, was arousing the authorities to deal
with the pauper and to dispose of the criminal
in such a way as to yield a profitable service to
the kingdom.   England was full of resolute men,
sea-dogs and soldiers of fortune, captains on the
land as well as the sea, who in times of peace were
seeking employment and profit and who needed an
outlet for their energies.   Some of these continued
in the service of kings and princes in Europe;
others conducted enterprises against the Spaniards
in the West Indies and along the Spanish Main;

while still others, such as John Smith and Miles
Standish, became pioneers in the work of English
colonization.

But more important than the promptings of
land-hunger and the desire for wealth and ad-
venture was the call made by a social and religious
movement which was but a phase of the general
restlessness and popular discontent. The Reformation, in which this movement had its origin,
was more than a revolt from the organization and
doctrines of the mediæval church; it voiced the
yearning of the middle classes for a position com-
mensurate with their growing prominence in
the national life. Though the feudal tenantry,
given over to agriculture and bound by the con-
ventions of feudal law, were still perpetuating
many of the old customs, the towns were emanci-
pating themselves from feudal control, and by
means of their wealth and industrial activities
were winning recognition as independent and
largely self-sufficing units. The gild, a closely
compacted brotherhood, existing partly for religious and educational purposes and partly for
the control of handicrafts and the exchange of
goods, became the center of middle-class energy,
and in thousands of instances hedged in the lives

of the humbler artisans. Thus it was largely from those who knew no wider world than the fields which they cultivated and the gilds which governed their standards and output that the early settlers of New England were recruited.

Equally important with the social changes were those which concerned men's faith and religious organization. The Peace of Augsburg, which in 1555 had closed for the moment the warfare resulting from the Reformation, not only recognized the right of Protestantism to exist, but also handed over to each state, whether kingdom, duchy, or principality, full power to control the creed within its borders. Whoever ruled the state could determine the religion of his subjects, a dictum which denied the right of individuals or groups of individuals to depart from the established faith. Hence arose a second revolt, not against the mediæval church and empire but against the authority of the state and its creed, whether Roman Catholic, Anglican, Lutheran, or Calvinist, a revolt in which Huguenot in France battled for his right to believe as he wished, and Puritan in England refused to conform to a manner of worship which retained much of the mediæval liturgy and ceremonial. Just as all great revolutionary movements in church or state give rise to men who repudiate tradition and all accretions due to human experience, and base their political and religious ideals upon the law of nature, the rights of man, the inner light, or the Word of God; so, too, in England under Elizabeth and James I, leaders appeared who demanded radical changes in faith and practice, and advocated complete separation from the Anglican Church and isolation from the religious world about them. Of such were the Separatists, who rejected the Anglican and other creeds, severed all bonds with a national church system, cast aside form, ceremony, liturgy, and a hierarchy of church orders, and sought for the true faith and form of worship in the Word of God. For these men the Bible was the only test of religious truth.

The Separatists organized themselves into small religious groups, as independent communities or companies of Christians, covenanted with God and keeping the Divine Law in a Holy Communion. They consisted in the main of men and women in the humbler walks of life — artisans, tenant farmers, with some middle-class gentry. Sufficient to themselves and knit together in the fashion of a gild or brotherhood, they believed in a church system of the simplest form and followed the Bible, Old and New Testaments alike, as the guide of their lives. Desiring to withdraw from the world as it was that they might commune together in direct relations with God, they accepted persecution as the test of their faith and welcomed hardship, banishment, and even death as proofs of righteousness and truth. Convinced of the scriptural soundness of what they believed and what they practised, and confident of salvation through unyielding submission to God's will as they interpreted it, they became conspicuous because of their radical thought and peculiar forms of worship, and inevitably drew upon themselves the attention of the authorities, both secular and ecclesiastical.

The leading centers of Separatism were in London and Norfolk, but the seat of the little congregation that eventually led the way across the sea to New England was in Scrooby in Nottinghamshire. There — in Scrooby manor-house, where William Brewster, the father, was receiver and bailiff, and his son, the future elder of the Plymouth colony, was acting postmaster; where Richard Clayton preached and John Robinson prayed; and where the youthful William Bradford was one of its members — there was gathered a small Separatist congregation composed of humble folk of Nottinghamshire and adjoining counties. They were soon discovered worshiping in the manor-house chapel, by the ecclesiastical authorities of Yorkshire, and for more than a year were subjected to persecution, some being "taken and clapt up in prison," others having "their houses besett and watcht night and day and hardly escaped their hands." At length they determined to leave England for Holland. During 1607 and 1608 they escaped secretly, some at one time, some at another, all with great loss and difficulty, until by the August of the latter year there were gathered at Amsterdam more than a hundred men, women, and children, "armed with faith and patience."

But Amsterdam proved a disappointing refuge. And in 1609 they moved to Leyden, "a fair and bewtifull citie," where for eleven years they remained, pursuing such trades as they could, chiefly weaving and the manufacture of cloth, "injoying much sweete and delightful societie and spiritual comfort togeather in the ways of God, under the able ministrie and prudente governmente of Mr. John Robinson and Mr.

William Brewster." But at last new and imperative reasons arose, demanding a third removal,
not to another city in Holland, but this time to
the New World called America. They were
breaking under the great labor and hard fare;
they feared to lose their language and saw no opportunity to educate their children; they disap-
proved of the lax Dutch observance of Sunday
and saw in the temptations of the place a menace
to the habits and morals of the younger members
of the flock, and, in the influences of the world
around them, a danger to the purity of their creed
and their practice. They determined to go to a
new country "devoyd of all civill inhabitants,"
where they might keep their names, their faith,
and their nationality.

After many misgivings, the fateful decision was
reached by the "major parte," and prepara-
tions for departure were made. But where to go
became a troublesome problem. The merits of
Guiana and other "wild coasts" were debated,
but finally Virginia met with general approval,
because there they might live as a private association, a distinct body by themselves, similar to
other private companies already established there.
To this end they sent two of their number to

England to secure a patent from the Virginia Company of London. Under this patent and in bond of allegiance to King James, yet acting as a "body in the most strict and sacred bond and covenant of the Lord," an independent and absolute church, they became a civil community also, with governors chosen for the work from among themselves. But the dissensions in the London Company caused them to lose faith in that association, and, hearing of the reorganization of the Virginia Company of Plymouth,[1] which about this time obtained a new charter as the New England Council, they turned from southern to northern Virginia — that is, to New England — and resolved to make their settlement where according to reports fishing might become a means of livelihood.

But their plans could not be executed without assistance; and, coming into touch with a London

[1] In 1606 King James had granted a charter incorporating two companies, one of which, made up of gentlemen and merchants in and about London, was known as the Virginia Company of London, the other as the Virginia Company of Plymouth. The former was authorized to plant colonies between thirty-four and forty-one degrees north latitude, and the latter between thirty-eight and forty-five, but neither was to plant a colony within one hundred miles of the other. Jamestown, the first colony of the London Company, was now thirteen years old. The Plymouth Company had made no permanent settlement in its domain.

merchant, Thomas Weston, who promised to aid
them, they entered into what proved to be a long
and wearisome negotiation with a group of adventurers — gentlemen, merchants, and others,
seventy in number — for an advance of money
to finance the expedition. The Pilgrims entered
into a partnership with the merchants to form
a voluntary joint-stock company. It was understood that the merchants, who purchased shares,
were to remain in England; that the colonists,
who contributed their personal service at a fixed
rating, were to go to America, there to labor at
trade, trucking, and fishing for seven years; and
that during this time all profits were to remain in
a common stock and all lands to be left undivided.
The conditions were hard and discouraging, but
there was no alternative; and at last, embarking at
Delfthaven in the *Speedwell*, a small ship bought
and fitted in Holland, they came to Southampton,
where another and larger vessel, the *Mayflower*,
was in waiting. In August, 1620, the two vessels
set sail, but the *Speedwell*, proving unseaworthy,
put back after two attempts, and the *Mayflower*
went on alone, bearing one hundred and two passengers, two-thirds of the whole, picked out as
worthy and willing to undertake the voyage.

The *Mayflower* reached the waters of New England on the 11th of November after a tedious course of sixty-five days from Plymouth to Cape Cod; but they did not decide on their place of landing until the 21st of December. Four days later they erected on the site of the town of Plymouth their first building.

The coast of New England was no unknown shore. During the years from 1607 to 1620, while settlers were founding permanent colonies at Jamestown and in Bermuda, explorers and fishermen, both English and French, had skirted its headlands and penetrated its harbors. In 1614, John Smith, the famous Virginia pioneer, who had left the service of the London Company and was in the employ of certain London merchants, had explored the northern coast in an open boat and had given the region its name. These many voyages and ventures at trading and fishing served to arouse enthusiasm in England for a world of good rivers and harbors, rich soil, and wonderful fishing, and to spread widely a knowledge of the coasts from Newfoundland to the Hudson River. Of this knowledge the Pilgrims reaped the benefit, and the captain of the *Mayflower*, Christopher Jones, against whom any charge of treachery may be dismissed, guided them, it is true, to a region unoccupied by Englishmen but not to one unknown or poorly esteemed. The miseries that confronted the Pilgrims during their first year in Plymouth colony were not due to the inhospitality of the region, but to the time of year when they landed upon it; and insufficiently provisioned as they were before they left England, it is little wonder that suffering and death should have accompanied their first experience with a New England winter.

This little group of men and women landed on territory that had been granted to the New England Council and they themselves had neither patent for their land nor royal authority to set up a government. But some form of government was absolutely necessary. Before starting from Southampton, they had followed Robinson's instructions to choose a governor and assistants for each ship "to order the people by the way"; and now that they were at the end of their long voyage, the men of the company met in the cabin of the *Mayflower*, and drew up a covenant in accordance with which they combined themselves together into a body politic for their better ordering and preservation. This compact, signed by forty-one members, of whom eleven bore the title of "Mister," was a plantation covenant, the political counterpart of the church covenant which bound together every Separatist community. It provided that the people should live together in a peaceable and orderly manner under civil authorities of their own choosing, and was the first of many such covenants entered into by New England towns, not defining a government but binding the settlers to unite politically as they had already done for religious worship. John Carver, who had been chosen governor on the *Mayflower*, was confirmed as governor of the settlement and given one assistant. After their goods had been set on shore and a few cottages built, the whole body "mette and consulted of lawes and orders, both for their civil and military governmente, still adding therunto as urgent occasion in severall times, and as cases did require."

Of this courageous but sorely stricken community more than half died before the first winter was over. But gradually the people became acclimated, new colonists came out, some from the community at Leyden, in the *Fortune*, the *Anne*, the *Charity*, and the *Handmaid*, and the numbers steadily increased. The settlers were in the

main a homogeneous body, both as to social class
and to religious views and purpose.   Among them
were undesirable members — some were sent out
by the English merchants and others came out of
their own accord — who played stool-ball on Sunday, committed theft, or set the community by the
ears, as did one notorious offender named Lyford.
But their number was not great, for most of them
remained but a short time, and then went to Virginia or elsewhere, or were shipped back to England by the Pilgrims as incorrigibles.   The life of
the people was predominantly agricultural, with
fishing, salt-making, and trading with the Indians
as allied interests.   The partners in England sent
overseas cattle, stock, and laborers, and, as their
profits depended on the success of the settlement,
did what they could to encourage its develop-
ment.   The position of the Pilgrims was that
of sharers and partners with the merchants,
from whom they received directions but not
commands.

But under the agreement of 1620 with their
partners in London, which remained in force for
seven years, the Plymouth people could neither
divide their land nor dispose of the products of
their labor, and so burdensome became this ar-

rangement that in 1623 temporary assignments of
land were made which in 1624 became permanent.
As Bradford said, and his comment is full of wisdom:

The experience that was had in this commone course
and condition, tried sundrie years, and that amongst
godly and sober men, may well evince the vanitie of
that conceite of Platos and other ancients, applauded
by some of later times; that the taking away of prop-
ertie, and bringing in communitie into a comone wealth,
would make them happy and florishing; as if they were
wiser then God. For this comunitie (so farr as it was)
was found to breed much confusion and discontent,
and retard much imployment that would have been
to their benefite and comforte. For the yong-men that
were most able and fitte for labour and service did re-
pine that they should spend their time and striength
to worke for other mens wives and children, with out
any recompence. The strong, or man of parts, had no
more in devission of victails and cloaths, than he
that was weake and not able to doe a quarter the other
could; this was thought injuestice. The aged and
graver men to be ranked and equalised in labours, and
victails, cloaths, etc., with the meaner and yonger
sorte, thought it some indignitie and disrespect unto
them. And for mens wives to be commanded to doe
servise for other men, as dresing their meate, washing
their cloaths, etc., they deemd it a kind of slaverie,
neither could many husbands well brooke it.

During the two years that followed, so evident
was the failure of the joint undertaking that

efforts were made on both sides to bring it to an
end; for the merchants, with no profit from the
enterprise, were anxious to avoid further indebted-
ness; and the colonists, wearying of the dual
control, wished to reap for themselves the full
reward of their own efforts. Under the new arrangement of small private properties, the settlers
began "to prise corne as more pretious than silver,
and those that had some to spare begane to trade
one with another for small things, by the quart,
potle, and peck, etc., for money they had none."
Later, finding "their corne, what they could
spare from ther necessities, to be a commoditie,
(for they sould it at 6s. a bushell) [they] used
great dilligence in planting the same. And the
Gov[erno]r and shuch as were designed to manage
the trade, (for it was retained for the generall
good, and none were to trade in particuler,) they
followed it to the best advantage they could; and
wanting trading goods, they understoode that a
plantation which was at Monhigen, and belonged
to some marchants of Plimoth [England] was to
breake up, and diverse usefull goods was ther
to be sould," the governor (Bradford himself)
and Edward Winslow "tooke a boat and some
hands and went thither. . . . With these goods,

and their corne after harvest they gott good store of trade, so as they were enabled to pay their ingagements against the time, and to get some cloathing for the people, and had some comodities beforehand." Though conditions were hard and often discouraging, the Pilgrims gradually found themselves self-supporting and as soon as this fact became clear, they sent Isaac Allerton to England "to make a composition with the adventurers." As a result of the negotiations an "agreement or bargen" was made whereby eight leading members of the colony bought the shares of the merchants for £1800 and distributed the payment among the settlers, who at this time numbered altogether about three hundred. Each share carried with it a certain portion of land and livestock. The debt was not finally liquidated until 1642.

By 1630, the Plymouth colony was fairly on its feet and beginning to grow in "outward estate." The settlers increased in number, prospered financially, and scattered to the outlying districts; and Plymouth the town and Plymouth the colony ceased to be identical. Before 1640, the latter had become a cluster of ten towns, each a covenanted community with its church and elder.

Though the colony never obtained a charter of incorporation from the Crown, it developed a form of government arising naturally from its own needs. By 1633 its governor and one assistant had become a governor and seven assistants, elected annually at a primary assembly held in Plymouth town; and the three parts, governor, assistants, and assembly, together constituted the governing body of the colony. In 1636, a revision of the laws and ordinances was made in the form of "The Great Fundamentals," a sort of constitution, frequently interspersed with statements of principles, which was printed with additions in 1671. The right to vote was limited at first to those who were members of the company and liable for its debt, but later the suffrage was extended to include others than the first-comers, and in 1633 was exercised by sixty-eight persons altogether. In 1668, a voter was required to have property, to be "of sober and peaceable conversation," and to take an oath of fidelity, but apparently he was never required to take the oath of allegiance to the Crown. So rapidly did the colony expand that, by 1639, the holding of a primary assembly in Plymouth town became so inconvenient that delegates had to be chosen.

Thus there was introduced into the colony a form of representative government, though it is to be noted that governor, assistants, and deputies sat together in a common room and never divided into two houses, as did the assemblies in other colonies.

The settlement of Plymouth colony is conspicuous in New England history because of the faith and courage and suffering of those who engaged in it and because of the ever alluring charm of William Bradford's *History of Plimouth Plantation*. The greatness of the Pilgrims lay in their illustrious example and in the influence they exercised upon the church life of the later New England colonies, for to the Pilgrims was due the fact that the congregational way of organization and worship became the accepted form in Massachusetts and Connecticut. But in other respects Plymouth was vastly overshadowed by her vigorous neighbors. Her people, humble and simple, were without importance in the world of thought, literature, or education. Their intellectual and material poverty, lack of business enterprise, unfavorable situation, and defenseless position in the eyes of the law rendered them almost a negative factor in the later life of New England. No great movement can be traced to their initiation, no great leader to birth within their borders, and no great work of art, literature, or scholarship to those who belonged to this unpretending company. The Pilgrim Fathers stand rather as an emblem of virtue than a moulding force in the life of the nation.

CHAPTER II

THE BAY COLONY

WHILE the Pilgrims were thus establishing themselves as the first occupants of the soil of New England, other men of various sorts and motives were trying their fortunes within its borders and were testing the opportunities which it offered for fishing and trade with the Indians. They came as individuals and companies, men of wandering disposition, romantic characters many of them, resembling the rovers and adventurers in the Caribbean or representing some of the many activities prevalent in England at the beginning of the seventeenth century. Thomas Weston, former ally of the Pilgrims, settled with a motley crew of rude fellows at Wessagusset (Quincy) and there established a trading post in 1622. Of this settlement, which came to an untimely end after causing the Pilgrims a great deal of trouble, only a blockhouse and stockade remained. Another irregular trader, Captain Wollaston, with some thirty or forty people, chiefly servants, established himself in 1625 two miles north of Wessagusset, calling the place Mount Wollaston. With him came that wit, versifier, and prince of roysterers, Thomas Morton, who, after Wollaston had moved on to Virginia, became "lord of misrule." Dubbing his seat Merrymount, drinking, carousing, and corrupting the Indians, affronting the decorous Separatists at Plymouth, Morton later became a serious menace to the peace of Massachusetts Bay. The Pilgrims felt that the coming of such adventurers and scoffers, who were none too scrupulous in their dealings with either white man or Indian and were given to practices which the Puritans heartily abhorred, was a calamity showing that even in the wilds of America they could not escape the world from which they were anxious to withdraw.

The settlements formed by these squatters and stragglers were quite unauthorized by the New England Council, which owned the title to the soil. As this Council had accomplished very little under its patent, Sir Ferdinando Gorges, its most active member, persisted in his efforts to found a colony, brought about a general distribution of the territory among its members, and obtained for himself and his son Robert, the section around and immediately north of Massachusetts Bay. An expedition was at once launched. In September, 1623, Robert Gorges with six gentlemen and a well-equipped and well-organized body of settlers reached Plymouth, — the forerunners, it was hoped, of a large number to come. This company of settlers was composed of families, the heads of which were mechanics and farmers, and with them were two clergymen, Morrell and Blackstone, the whole constituting the greatest enterprise set on foot in America by the Council. Robert Gorges, bearing a commission constituting him Governor-General over all New England, made his settlement at Weston's old place at Wessagusset. Here he built houses and stored his goods and began the founding of Weymouth, the second permanent habitation in New England and the first on Massachusetts Bay. Unfortunately, famine, that arch-enemy of all the early settlers, fell upon his company, his father's resources in England proved inadequate, and he and others were obliged to return. Of those that remained a few stayed at Wessagusset; one of the clergymen, William Blackstone, with his wife went to Shawmut (Boston); Samuel Maverick and his wife, to Winnissimmet

(Chelsea); and the Walfords, to Mishawum (Charlestown). Probably all these people were Anglicans; some later became freemen of the Massachusetts colony; others who refused to conform returned to England; but Blackstone remained in his little cottage on the south slope of Beacon Hill, unwilling to join any of the churches, because, as he said, he came from England to escape the "Lord Bishops," and he did not propose in America to be under the "Lord Brethren."

The colony of Massachusetts Bay began as a fishing venture with profit as its object. It so happened that the Pilgrims wished to secure a right to fish off Cape Ann, and through one of their number they applied to Lord Sheffield, a member of the Council who had shared in the distribution of 1623. Sheffield caused a patent to be drawn, which the Plymouth people conveyed to a Dorchester company desiring to establish a fishing colony in New England. The chief promoter of the Dorchester venture was the Reverend John White, a conforming Puritan clergyman, in whose congregation was one John Endecott. The company thus organized remained in England but sent some fourteen settlers to Cape Ann in the winter of 1623–1624. Fishing and planting, however, did not go well together, the venture failed, and the settlers removed southward to Naumkeag (Salem). Though many of the English company desired to abandon the undertaking, there were others, among whom were a few Puritans or Non-conformists, who favored its continuance. These men consulted with others of like mind in London, and through the help of the Earl of Warwick, a nobleman friendly to the Puritan cause, a patent was issued by the Council to Endecott and five associates, for land extending from above the Merrimac to below the Charles. This patent, it will be noticed, included the territory already granted to Gorges and his son Robert, and was obtained apparently with the consent of Gorges, who thought that his own and his son's rights would be safely protected. Under this patent, the partners sent over Endecott as governor with sixty others to begin a colony at Salem, where the "old planters" from Cape Ann had already established themselves. Salem was thus a plantation from September, 1628, to the summer of 1630, on land granted to the associates in England; and the relations of these two were much the same as those of Jamestown with the London Company.

Endecott and his associates soon made it evident, however, that they were planning larger things for themselves and had no intention, if they could help it, of recognizing the claims of Gorges and his son. They wanted complete control of their territory in New England, and to this end they applied to the Crown for a confirmation of their land-patent and for a charter of incorporation as a company with full powers of government. As this application was a deliberate defiance of Gorges and the New England Council, it has always been a matter of surprise that the associates were able to gain the support of the Crown in this effort to oust Gorges and his son from lands that were legally theirs. No satisfactory explanation has ever been advanced, but it is worthy of note that at this juncture Gorges was in France in the service of the King, whereas on the side of the associates and their friends was the Earl of Warwick, himself deeply interested in colonizing projects and one of the most powerful men in England. The charter was obtained March 4, 1629 — how, we do not know. It created a corporation of twenty-six members, Anglicans and Nonconformists, known as the Massachusetts Bay Company.

But if the original purpose of this company was

to engage in a business enterprise for the sake of profit, it soon underwent a noteworthy transformation. In 1629, control passed into the hands of those members of the company in whom a religious motive was uppermost. How far the charter was planned at first as a Puritan contrivance to be used in case of need will never be known. It is equally uncertain whether the particular form of charter, with the place of the company's residence omitted, was selected to facilitate a possible removal of the company from England to America; but it is likely that removal was early in the minds of the Puritan members of the company. At this time a great many people felt as did the Reverend John White, who expressed the hope that God's people should turn with eyes of longing to the free and open spaces of the New World, whither they might flee to be at peace. But, when the charter was granted, the Puritans were not in control of the company, which remained in England for a year after it was incorporated, superintending the management of its colony just as other trading companies had done.

But events were moving rapidly in England. Between March, 1629, and March, 1630, Parliament was dissolved under circumstances of great excitement, parliamentary privileges were set aside, parliamentary leaders were sent to the Tower, and the period of royal rule without Parliament began. The heavy hand of an autocratic government fell on all those within reach who upheld the Puritan cause, among whom was John Winthrop, a country squire, forty-one years of age, who was deprived of his office as attorney in the Court of Wards. Disillusioned as to life in England because of financial losses and family bereavements, and now barred from his customary employment by act of the Government, he turned his thoughts toward America. Acting with the approval of the Earl of Warwick and in conjunction with a group of Puritan friends — Thomas Dudley, Isaac Johnson, Richard Saltonstall, and John Humphrey,— he decided in the summer of 1629 to leave England forever, and in September he joined the Massachusetts Bay Company. Almost immediately he showed his capacity for leadership, was soon elected governor, and was able during the following winter to obtain such a control of affairs as to secure a vote in favor of the transfer of charter and company to New England. The official organization was remodeled so that only those desiring to remove should be in con-

trol, and on March 29, 1630, the company
with its charter, accompanied by a considerable
number of prospective colonists, set sail from
Cowes near the Isle of Wight in four vessels,
the *Arabella,* the *Talbot,* the *Ambrose,* and the
Jewel, the remaining passengers following in
seven other vessels a week or two later. The
voyages of the vessels were long, none less than
nine weeks, by way of the Azores and the Maine
coast, and the distressed Puritans, seven hundred
altogether, scurvy-stricken and reduced in numbers by many deaths, did not reach Salem until
June and July. Hence they moved on to Charlestown, set up their tents on the slope of the hill,
and on the 23rd of August, held the first official
meeting of the company on American soil; but finding no running water in the place and still pursued
by sickness and death, they again removed, this
time to Boston, where they built houses against the
winter. With the founding of this colony — the
colony of Massachusetts Bay — a new era for New
England began.

This grant of territory to the Massachusetts
Bay Company and of the charter confirming the
title and conveying powers of government put a
complete stop to Gorges's plans for a final proprie-

torship in New England.   Gorges had acquiesced
in the first grant by the New England Council
because he thought it a sub-grant, like that to
Plymouth, in no way injuring his own control.
But when in 1632, he learned the true inwardness
of the Massachusetts title and discovered that
Warwick and the Puritans had outwitted him by
obtaining royal confirmation of a grant that ex-
tinguished his own proprietary rights, he turned
on Warwick, declared that the charter had been
surreptitiously obtained, and demanded that it
be brought to the Council board.   Learning that
it had gone to New England, he forced the withdrawal of Warwick from the Council, and from
that time forward for five years bent all his efforts
to overthrow the Puritan colony by obtaining the
annulment of its privileges.

In this attempt, he was aided by Captain John
Mason, an able, energetic promoter of colonizing
movements who had already been concerned with
settlements in Newfoundland and Nova Scotia, and
who was zealous to begin a plantation in the province of Maine.   Mason had received grants from
the Council, both individually and in partnership
with Gorges, and had visited New England in the
interest of his claims.   Through the influence of

Gorges, he was now made a member of the Council and joined in the movement to break the hold of the Puritans upon New England. He and Gorges found useful allies in three men who had been driven out of Massachusetts by the Puritan leaders soon after their arrival at Boston — Thomas Morton of Merrymount, Sir Christopher Gardiner, a picturesque, somewhat mysterious personage thought to have been an agent of Gorges in New England, with methods and morals that gave offense to Massachusetts, and Philip Ratcliffe, a much less worthy character given to scandal and invective, who had been deprived of his ears by the Puritan authorities. These men were bitter in their denunciation of the Puritan government.

The situation was perilous for the new colony, which was hardly yet firmly established. In direct violation of the royal commands, hundreds of men and women were leaving England — not merely adventurers or humble Separatists, but sober people of the better classes, of mature years and substantial characters. When, therefore, Gorges and the others meeting at Gorges's house at Plymouth brought their complaints to the attention of the Privy Council, they were listened to with attention, and instructions were sent at once to stop the Puritan ships and to bring the charter of the Massachusetts Company to the Council board. To check the Puritan migration and to institute further inquiry into the facts of the case a commission was appointed in 1634, with Archbishop Laud at its head, for the special purpose, among others, of revoking charters "surreptitiously and unduly obtained." Gorges and Morton appealed to Laud against the Puritans, and Morton wrote his *New England Canaan*, which he dedicated to Laud, in the hope of exposing the motives of the colony and of arousing the Archbishop to action. Warwick threw his influence on the side of Massachusetts, being always forward, as Winthrop said, "to do good to our colony"; and the colony itself, fearing attack, began to fortify Castle Island in the harbor and to prepare for defense. Endecott, in wrath, defaced the royal ensign at Salem, and so intense was the excitement and so determined the attitude of the Puritans that, had the Crown attempted to send over a Governor-General or to seize the charter by force, the colony would have resisted to the full extent of its power.

Gorges, believing that he could work better through the King and the Archbishop than through the New England Council, brought about the dis-

JOHN WINTHROP

Painting by Charles Osgood, 1834, copied from the original in the State House, Boston. In the collection of the Massachusetts Historical Society, Boston.

solution of that body in 1635, thus making it possible for the King to deal directly with the New England situation. Before its dissolution the Council had authorized Morton, acting as its lawyer, to bring the case to the attention of the Attorney-General of England, who filed in the Court of King's Bench a complaint against Massachusetts, as a result of which a writ of *quo warranto* was issued against the Company.

The outlook was ominous for Puritanism, not only in New England but in old England as well. That year saw the flight of the greatest number of emigrants across the sea, for the persecution in England was at its height, the Puritan aristocracy was suffering in its estates, and Puritan divines were everywhere silenced or dismissed. Even Warwick was shorn of a part of his power. Young Henry Vane, son of a baronet, had already gone to America, and such men as Lord Saye and Sele, Lord Brooke, and Sir Arthur Haslerigg were thinking of migrating and had prepared a refuge at Saybrook where they might find peace. But the turn of the tide soon came. The royal Government was bankrupt, the resistance to the payment of ship-money was already making itself felt, and disturbances in the central and eastern counties were absorbing the attention and energies of the Government. Gorges, left alone to execute the writ against the colony, joined with Mason in building a ship for the purpose of carrying the *quo warranto* to New England, but the vessel broke in the launching, and their resources were at an end. Mason died in 1635, and Gorges, an old man of seventy, bankrupt and discouraged, could do no more. Though Morton continued the struggle, and though, in 1638, the Committee of the Council for Foreign Plantations (the Laud Commission) again demanded the charter, the danger was past: conditions in England had become so serious for the King that the complaints against Massachusetts were lost to view. At last in 1639 Gorges obtained his charter for a feudal propriety in Maine but no further attempts were made to overthrow the Massachusetts Bay colony.

During the years from 1630 to 1640, the growth of the colony was extraordinarily rapid. In the first year alone seventeen ships with two thousand colonists came over, and it is estimated that by 1641 three hundred vessels bearing twenty thousand passengers had crossed the Atlantic. It was a great migration. Inevitably many went back, but the great majority remained and settled in

Boston and its neighborhood — Roxbury, Charlestown, Dorchester, Cambridge, and Watertown,
where in 1643 were situated according to Winthrop "near half of the commonwealth for number
of people and substance." From the first the colonists dispersed rapidly, establishing in favorable
places settlements which they generally called plantations but sometimes towns. In these they lived
as petty religious and civil communities, each under
its minister, with civil officials chosen from among
themselves. In the decade following 1630 the number of such settlements rose to twenty-two. The
inhabitants were almost purely English in stock,
with here and there an Irishman, a few Jews, and
an occasional negro from the West Indies. Nearly
all the settlers were of Puritan sympathies, and of
middle-class origin — tenants from English estates,
artisans from English towns, and many inden-
tured servants. A few were of the aristocracy, such
as Lady Arabella Johnson, daughter of the Earl
of Lincoln, Sir Richard Saltonstall, Lady Deborah Moody, members of the Harlakenden
family, young Henry Vane, Thomas Gorges,
and a few others. Of "Misters" and "Es-
quires" there was a goodly number, such as
Winthrop, Haynes, Emanuel Downing, and the

like. The first leaders were exceptional men, possessed of ability and education, and many were university graduates, who brought with them the books and the habits of the reader and scholar of their day. They were superior to those of the second and third generation in the breadth of their ideas and in the vigor and origin-ality of their convictions.

Migration ceased in 1641, and a time of stress and suffering set in. Commodities grew scarce, prices rose, many colonists returned to England leaving debts behind, and as yet the colony pro-duced no staples to exchange for merchandise from the mother country. Some of the settlers, dis-couraged, went to the West Indies; others, fleeing for fear of want, found their way to the Dutch at Long Island. Pressure was brought to bear at various times to persuade the people to migrate elsewhere as a body, to Old Providence and Trini-dad in the Caribbean, to Maryland, and later to Jamaica; but these attempts proved vain. The Puritan was willing to endure hardship and suffer-ing for the sake of civil and religious independence, but he was not willing to lose his identity among those who did not share his faith in the guiding hand of God or who denied the principles according to which he wished to govern his community. At first the leaders of the migration were Non-conformists not Separatists. Francis Higginson, Endecott's minister at Salem, had declared in 1629 that they did not go to New England as separatists from the Church of England but only as those who would "separate from the corruption in it"; and Winthrop used "Easter" and the customary names of the months until 1635. But the Puritans became essentially Separatists from the day when Dr. Samuel Fuller of Plymouth persuaded the Salem community, even before the company itself had left England, to accept the practices of the Plymouth Church. Each town consequently had its church, pastor, teacher, and covenant, and became an independent Congregational community — a circumstance which left a deep impress upon the life and history of New England.

The government of the colony was never a democracy in the modern sense of the term. At first in 1630, control was assumed by the governor and his assistants, leaving but little power in the hands of the freeman; but such usurpation of power could not last, and in 1632 the freemen were given the right to elect officials, to make and enforce laws, raise money, impose taxes, and dispose of lands. Thus was begun the transformation of the court of the company into a parliament, and the company itself into a commonwealth. So self-sufficient did the colony become in these early years of its history that by 1646 Massachusetts could assert that it owed only allegiance to England and was entirely independent of the British Parliament in all matters of government, in which affairs under its charter it had absolute power. Many denied this contention of the leaders, asserting that the company was only a corporation and that any colonist had a right of appeal to England. Winthrop refused definitely to recognize this right, and measures were taken to purge the colony of these refractory spirits, among whom were Dr. Robert Child, one of the best educated men of the colony, William Vassall, and Samuel Maverick. All were fined, some clapped in irons, and many banished. Child returned to England, Vassall went to Barbados, and the rest were silenced. So menacing was the revolt that Edward Winslow was sent to England to present the case to the parliamentary commissioners, which he did successfully.

But among those who upheld the freedom of

the colony from English interference and control there were many who complained of the form the government was taking. The franchise was limited to church members, which debarred five-sixths of the population from voting and holding office; the magistrates insisted on exercising a negative vote upon the proceedings of the deputies, because they deemed it necessary to prevent the colony from degenerating into "a mere democracy"; and the ministers or elders exercised an influence in purely civil matters that rendered them arbiters in all disputes between the magistrates and the deputies. Until 1634, the general court had been a primary assembly, but in that year representation was introduced and the towns sent deputies, who soon began to complain of the meagerness of their powers. From this time on, the efforts of the deputies to reduce the authority of the magistrates and to increase their own were continuous and insistent. One bold dissenter was barred from public office in 1635 for daring to deny the magistrates' claim, and others expressed their fear that autocratic rule and a governor for life would endanger the liberty of the people. The dominance of the clergy tended to the maintenance of an intolerant theocracy and was offensive to many in Massachusetts who, having fled from Laud's intolerance at home, had no desire to submit to an equal intolerance in New England. Between 1634 and 1638 the manifestations of this dislike became conspicuous and alarming. The Governor's son, the younger John Winthrop, dissatisfied with the hard régime in Massachusetts, returned to England in 1634. Henry Vane, though elected Governor in 1636, showed marked discontent, and when defeated the next year left the colony. The English aristocratic Puritans, Saye and Sele, Brooke, and others, who planned to leave England in 1635, found themselves so out of accord with the Massachusetts policy of limiting of the suffrage to church members — and to church membership as determined by the clergy — that they refused to go to Boston, and persisted in their plan for a settlement at Saybrook. The Massachusetts system had thus become not a constitutional government fashioned after the best liberal thought in England of that day, but a narrow oligarchy in which the political order was determined according to a rigid interpretation of theology. This excessive theocratic concentration of power resulted in driving from the colony many of its best men.

More notorious even than the political dissensions were the moral and theological disputes which almost disrupted the colony. The magistrates and elders did not compel men to leave the colony because of political heresy, but they did drive them out because of difference in matters of theology. Even before the company came over, Endecott had sent John and Samuel Browne back to England because they worshiped according to the Book of Common Prayer. Morton and six others were banished in 1630 as an immoral influence. Sir Christopher Gardiner, Philip Ratcliffe, Richard Wright, the Walfords, and Henry Lynn were all forced to leave in 1630 and 1631 as "unmeete to inhabit here." Roger Williams, the tolerationist and upholder of soulliberty, who complained of the magistrates for oppression and of the elders for injustice and who opposed the close union of church and state, was compelled to leave during the winter of 1635 and 1636. But the great expulsion came in 1637, when an epidemic of heresy struck the colony. A synod at Newtown condemned eighty erroneous opinions, and the general court then disarmed or banished all who persisted in error.

A furor of excitement gathered about Anne

Hutchinson, who claimed to be moved by the spirit and denied that an outward conformity to the letter of the covenant was a sufficient test of true religion unless accompanied with a change in the inner life. She was a nonconformist among those who, refusing to conform to the Church of England, had now themselves become conformists of the strictest type. To Mrs. Hutchinson the "vexatious legalism of Puritanism" was as abhorrent as had been the practices of the Roman and Anglican churches to the Puritans, and, though the latter did not realize it, they were as unjust to her as Laud had been to them. She broke from a covenant of works in favor of a covenant of grace and in so doing defied the standing authorities and the ruling clergy of the colony. Her wit, undeniable power of exhortation, philanthropic disposition, and personal attributes which gave her an ascendency in the Boston church, drew to her a large following and placed the supremacy of the orthodox party in peril. After a long and wordy struggle to check the "misgovernment of a woman's tongue" and to rebuke "the impudent boldness of a proud dame," Mrs. Hutchinson was excommunicated and banished; and certain of those who upheld her — Wheelwright, Coggeshall,

Aspinwall, Coddington, and Underhill, all leading
men of the colony — were also forced to leave. In
Boston and the adjoining towns dozens of men were
disarmed for fear of a general uprising against the
orthodox government.

This discord put a terrible strain on the colony,
and one marvels that it weathered the storm.
Only an iron discipline that knew neither charity
nor tolerance could have successfully resisted the
attacks on the standing order. The years from
1635 to 1638 were a critical time in the history
of the colony, and the unyielding attitude of
magistrates and elders was due in no small part
to the danger of attack from England. Determined, on the one hand, to save the colony from
the menace of Anglican control, and, on the other,
to prevent the admission of liberal and democratic
ideas, they struggled to maintain the rule of a
minority in behalf of a precise and logically defined theocratic system that admitted neither
experiment nor compromise. For the moment
they were successful, because the Cromwellian
victory in England was favorable to their cause.
But should independence be overthrown at home,
should religion cease to be a deciding factor in
political quarrels, and should the monarchy and

the Established Church gain ascendency once more, then Massachusetts would certainly reap the whirlwind.   The harvesting might be long but the garnering would be none the less sure.

CHAPTER III

THROUGH the portal of Boston at one time or another passed all or nearly all those who were to found additional colonies in New England; and from that portal, willingly or unwillingly, men and women journeyed north, south, and west, searching for favorable locations, buying land of the Indians, and laying the groundwork for permanent homes and organized communities. In this way were begun the colonies of Rhode Island, Connecticut, New Haven, and New Hampshire, each of which sprang in part from the desire for separate religious and political life and in part from the migratory instinct which has always characterized the Englishman in his effort to find a home and a means of livelihood. Sometimes individuals wandered alone or in groups of two or three, but more frequently covenanted companies of men and women of like minds moved

45

across the face of the land, followed Indian trails, or voyaged by water along the coast and up the rivers, usually remaining where they first found satisfaction, but often, in new combinations, taking up the burden of their journeying and moving on, a second, a third, and even a fourth time in search of homes. Abraham Pierson and his flock migrated four times in thirty years, seeking a place where they might find rest under a government according to God.

The frontier Puritan was neither docile nor easily satisfied. He was restless, opinionated, and eager to assert himself and his convictions. The controversies among the elect regarding doctrines and morals often became so heated that complete separation was the only remedy; and wherever there was a migrating leader followers were sure to be found. Hence, despite the dangers from cold, famine, the Indian, and the wilderness, the men of New England were constantly shifting in these earlier years as one motive or another urged them on. Land was plentiful, and, as a rule, easily obtained; opportunities for trade presented themselves to any one who would seek them; and the freedom of earth and sky and of nature unspoiled offered an ideal environment for a closer communion with God. Owing to the many varieties of religious opinion that prevailed among these radical pioneers, each new grouping and consequent settlement had an individuality of its own, determined by the personality of its leader and by the ideas that he represented. Thus Williams, Clarke, Coddington, and Gorton influenced Rhode Island; Hooker, Haynes, and Ludlow, Connecticut; Davenport, Eaton, and Pierson, New Haven; and Wheelwright and Underhill, New Hampshire.

Roger Williams, the founder of Providence — the first plantation to be settled in what was later the colony of Rhode Island — was driven out of Boston because he called in question the authority of the government, denied the legality of its land title as derived from the King, and contested the right of the magistrates to deal with matters ecclesiastical. Making his way through the wilderness in the winter of 1635–1636, he finally settled on the Mooshassuc River, calling the place Providence; and in the ensuing two years he gathered about him a number of those who found the church system of Massachusetts intolerable and the Erastian doctrines of the magistrates, according to which the sins of believers were to be punished by civil authority, distressing to their consciences. They drew up a plantation covenant, promising to subject themselves "in active or passive obedience to all such orders or agreements" as might be made for the public good in an orderly way by the majority vote of the masters of families, "incorporated together into a town fellowship," but "only in civill things." Thus did the men of Providence put into practice their doctrine of a church separable from the state, and of a political order in which there were no magistrates, no elders exercising civil as well as spiritual authority, and no restraint on soul liberty.

A year or two later William Coddington, loyal ally of Anne Hutchinson, with others — Clarke, Coggeshall, and Aspinwall, who resented the aggressive attitude of Boston — purchased from the Indians the island of Aquidneck in Narragansett Bay and at the northern end planted Pocasset, afterwards Portsmouth, the second settlement in the colony of Rhode Island. They, too, entered into a covenant to join themselves into a body politic and elected Coddington as their judge and five others as elders. But this modeling of the government after the practices of the Old Testament

was not pleasing to a majority of the community, which desired a more democratic organization. After a few months, in the spring of 1639, Coddington and his followers therefore journeyed southward and established a third settlement at Newport. Here the members adopted a covenant, "engaging" themselves "to bear equall charges, answerable to our strength and estates in common," and to be governed "by major voice of judge and elders; the judge to have a double voice." Though differing from the system as developed in Massachusetts, the Newport government at the beginning had a decidedly theocratic character.

The last of the Rhode Island settlements was at Shawomet, or Warwick, on the western mainland at the upper end of the Bay. There Samuel Gorton, the mystic and transcendentalist, one of the most individual of men in an era of striking individualities, after many vicissitudes found an abiding place. He was of London, "a clothier and professor of the misteries of Christ," a believer in established authority as the surest guardian of liberty, and an opponent of formalism in all its varieties. Arriving at Boston in 1637 at the height of the Hutchinsonian controversy, he had sought liberty of conscience, first in Boston, then

4

in Plymouth, and finally in Portsmouth, where he had become a leader after the withdrawal of Coddington. But in each place his instinct for justice and his too vociferous denial of the legality of verdicts rendered by self-constituted authorities led him to seek further for a home that would shelter him and his followers. No sooner, however, was he settled at Shawomet, than the Massachusetts authorities laid claim to the territory, and it was only after arrest, imprisonment, and a narrow escape from the death penalty, followed by a journey to England and the enlisting of the sympathies of the Earl of Warwick, that he made good his claim.   Gorton returned in 1648 with a letter from Warwick, as Lord Admiral and head of the parliamentary commission on plantation affairs, ordering Massachusetts to cease molesting him and his people, and he named the plantation Warwick after his patron,

Samuel Gorton played an influential and useful part in the later history of the colony, and his career of peaceful service to Rhode Island belies the opinion, based on Winslow's partisan pamphlet, *Hypocrasie Unmasked*, and other contemporary writings, that he was a blasphemer, a "crude and half-crazy thinker," a "proud and pestilent seducer," and a "most prodigious minter of exorbitant novelties." He preferred "the universitie of humane reason and reading of the volume of visible creation" to sectarianism and convention. No wonder the Massachusetts leaders could not comprehend him! He questioned their infallibility, their ecclesiastical caste, and their theology, and for their own self-preservation they were bound to resist what they deemed his heresies.

Thus Rhode Island at the beginning was formed of four separate and independent communities, each in embryo a petty state, no one of which possessed at first other than an Indian title for its lands and a self-made plantation covenant as the warrant for its government. To settle disputes over land titles and to dispose of town lands, Providence established in 1640 a court of arbitration consisting of five "disposers," who seem also to have served as a sort of executive board for the town. In all outward relations she remained isolated from her neighbors, pursuing a course of strictly local independence. Portsmouth and Newport, for the sake of greater strength, united in March, 1640, and a year later agreed on a form of government which they called "a democratic or popular government," in which none was to be "accounted a delinquent for doctrine." They set up a governor, deputy governor, and four assistants, regularly elected, and provided that all laws should be made by the freemen or the major part of them, "orderly assembled." In the system thus established we can see the influence of the older colonies and the beginning of a stronger government, but at best the experiment was half-hearted, for each town reserved to itself complete control over its own affairs. In 1647 Portsmouth withdrew "to be as free in their transactions as any other town in the colony," and the spirit of separatism was still dominant.

But it soon became necessary for the four towns of what is now Rhode Island to have something more legal upon which to base their right to exist than a title derived from their plantation covenants and Indian bargains. Massachusetts was extending her claims southward; Edward Winslow was in England ready to show that the Rhode Island settlements were within the bounds of the Plymouth patent; and certain individuals, traders and land-seekers, were locating in the Narragansett country and taking possession of the soil. To combat these claims, Roger Williams, who had so vehemently denied the validity of a royal patent a few years before, but influenced now, it may be, by Gorton's insistence that a legal title could be obtained only from England, sailed overseas and secured from the parliamentary commissioners in March, 1644, a charter uniting Providence, Portsmouth, and Newport, under the name of Providence Plantations in the Narragansett Bay, and granting them powers of government. For the moment even this document had no certain value, for, in spite of the fact that the parliamentarians were at war with the King, Charles I was still sovereign of England and should he win in the Civil War the title would be worthless. However, the patent was not put in force until 1647, after the victory of Cromwell at Naseby had given control into the hands of Parliament; and then a general meeting was held at Portsmouth consisting of the freemen of Warwick, Portsmouth, and Newport, and ten representatives from Providence. The patent did not state how affairs were to be managed, and the colonials, meeting in subsequent assemblies, worked out the problem in their own way. They refused to have a governor, and, creating only a presiding officer with four assistants, constituted a court of trials for the hearing of important criminal and civil causes.   No general court was created by law, but a legislative body soon came into existence consisting of six deputies from each town.   Before this Portsmouth meeting of 1647 adjourned, it adopted a code of laws in which witchcraft trials and imprisonment for debt were forbidden, capital punishment was largely abolished, and divorce was granted for adultery only.   In 1652, the assembly passed a noteworthy law against the holding of negroes in slavery.

But the new patent did not bring peace to the colony.   In 1649, Roger Williams wrote to Governor Winthrop: "Our poor colony is in civil dissension.   Their last meeting [of the assembly] at which I have not been, have fallen into factions.   Mr. Coddington and Captain Partridge, etc., are the heads of one, and Captain Clarke, Mr. Easton, etc., the heads of the other."   What had happened was this.   Coddington, representing the conservative and theocratic wing of the assembly and opposing those who were more liberally minded, had evidently applied to Massachusetts and Plymouth for support in the effort to obtain an independent government for Aquidneck. This plan would have destroyed what unity the colony had obtained under the patent, but Coddington wished to be governor of a colony of his own. Both Massachusetts and Plymouth were favorable to this plan, as they hoped to further their own claims to the territory of islands and mainland. Twice Coddington made application to the newly formed Confederation of New England for admission, but was refused unless he would bring in Aquidneck as part of Massachusetts or Plymouth, the latter of which laid claim to it. Coddington himself was willing to do this but found the opposition to the plan so vehement that he gave up the attempt and went to England to secure a patent of his own. After long negotiations he was successful in his quest and returned with a document which appointed him governor for life with almost viceregal powers. But he had reckoned without the people whom he was to govern. Learning of the outcome of Coddington's mission and hearing that he had had secret dealings also with the Dutch at New Amsterdam, the inhabitants of the islands rose in revolt, hanged Captain Partridge and compelled Coddington to seek safety in flight. Williams again went to England in 1651 and procured the recall of Coddington's commission and a confirmation of his own patent, and Coddington in 1656 gave in his submission and was forgiven.

The early history of Rhode Island thus furnishes a remarkable exhibition of intense individualism in things religious and a warring of disruptive forces in matters of civil organization.

Connecticut was settled during the years 1634 to 1636 by people from Massachusetts. Knowledge of the fertile Connecticut valley had come early to the Dutch, who had planted a block-house, the House of Good Hope, at the southeast corner of the land upon which Hartford now stands. Plymouth, too, in searching for advantageous trade openings had sent out one William Holmes, who sailed past the Dutch fort and took possession of the site of Windsor. In the autumn of 1634 a certain John Oldham, trader and rover and frequent disturber of the Puritan peace, came with a few companions and began to occupy and cultivate lands within the bounds of modern Wethersfield. Settlers continued to arrive from Massachusetts, either by land or by water, actuated by land-hunger and stirred to movement westward by the same driving impulse that for years to come was to populate the frontier wherever it stretched. The territory thus possessed was claimed at first by Massachusetts, on the theory that the southern line of the colony, if ex-

tended westward, would include this portion of
the Connecticut River. It was also claimed by
the group of English lords and gentlemen, Saye
and Sele, Brooke, and other Puritans, who, as
they supposed, had obtained through the Earl
of Warwick from the New England Council a
grant of land extending west and southwest from
Narragansett Bay forty leagues. These claims
were of course irreconcilable, but the English lords,
in order to assert their title, sent over in 1635 twenty
servants, known as the Stiles party, who reached
Connecticut in the summer of that year. Thus
by autumn there were on the ground four sets
of rival claimants: the Dutch, the Plymouth
traders, various emigrants from Massachusetts,
chiefly from the town of Dorchester, and the
Stiles party, representing the English lords and
gentlemen. Their relations were not harmonious,
for the Dutch tried to drive out the Plymouth
traders, and the latter resented in their turn the
attempt of the Dorchester men to occupy their
lands.

The matter was to be settled not by force but
by weight of numbers and soundness of title.
In 1635, a new and larger migration was under
consideration in Massachusetts, prompted by

various motives: partly personal, as shown in
the rivalries of strong men in a colony already
overstocked with leaders; partly material, as
indicated by the desire for wider fields for culti-
vation and especially good pasture; and partly
political, as evidenced by the dislike on the part
of many for the power of the elders and magistrates
in Massachusetts and by the strong inclination of
masterful men toward a government of their own.
Thomas Hooker, the pastor of the Newtown
church, John Haynes, the Governor of Massachusetts in 1635, and Roger Ludlow, a former magistrate and deputy governor who had failed of
election to the magistracy in the same year, were
the leaders of the movement and, if we may judge
from later events, were believers in certain political
ideas that were not finding application in the Bay
Colony. Disappointed because of the rigidity of
the Massachusetts system, they seem to have
waited for an opportunity to put into practice
the principles which they believed essential to the
true government of a people.

When the decision was finally reached and
certain of the inhabitants of Newtown, Watertown, and Roxbury were ready to enter on their
removal, the question naturally arose as to the

title to the territory. In June, 1635, Massachusetts had asserted her claim by exercising a sort
of supervision over those who had already gone to
Connecticut; but in October John Winthrop, Jr.,
the Reverend Hugh Peters, and Henry Vane arrived from England with authority from the lords
and gentlemen to push their claim, and Winthrop
actually bore a commission as governor of the entire territory, which included Connecticut. It is
hardly possible that Hooker and Haynes would
have ignored the demands of these agents, and yet
to acknowledge Winthrop as their governor would
have been to accept a head who was not of their
own choosing. In all probability some arrangement was made with Winthrop, according to
which the Englishmen's title to the lands was
recognized but at the same time the Connecticut
settlers were to have full powers of self-government, and the question of a governor was left for
the moment undecided, Winthrop confining his
jurisdiction to Saybrook, the settlement which
he was to promote at the mouth of the river.
This agreement was embodied in a commission
which was drawn up by the Massachusetts General
Court and issued in March, 1636, "on behalf of
our said members and John Winthrop, Jr.," and

was to last for one year. Who actually wrote this commission we do not know, but the Connecticut men said afterwards that it arose from the desire of the people who removed, because they did not want to go away without a frame of government agreed on beforehand and did not want to recognize "any claymes of the Massachusetts jurisdiction over them by vertew of Patent." Apparently the people going to Connecticut wanted to get as far away from Massachusetts as possible.

Armed with their commission, in the summer of 1636, members of the Newtown church to the number of about one hundred persons, led by Thomas Hooker, their pastor, and Samuel Stone, his assistant, made a famous pilgrimage under summer skies through the woods that lay between Massachusetts and the Connecticut River. Bearing Mrs. Hooker in a litter and driving their cattle before them, these courageous pioneers, men, women, and children, after a fortnight's journeying, reached Hartford, the site of their future home, already occupied by those who had foregathered there in number larger even than those who had newly arrived. At about the same time, William Pynchon and others of Roxbury, acting from similar motives, took the same course westward, but instead of continuing down the Connecticut River, as the others had done, stopped at its banks and made their settlement at Agawam (Springfield), where they built a warehouse and a wharf for use in trade with the Indians. The lower settlements, Hartford, Wethersfield, and Windsor, became agricultural communities; but Springfield, standing at the junction of Indian trails and river communication, was destined to become the center of the beaver trade of the region, shipping furs and receiving commodities through Boston, either in shallops around the Cape or on pack-horses overland by the path the emigrants had trod. Pynchon's settlement was one of the towns named in the commission and, for the first year after it was founded, joined with the others in maintaining order in the colony.

The commission government came to an end in March, 1637, and there is reason to think that during the last month, an election of committees took place in Hartford, Wethersfield, and Windsor, which would show that the Connecticut settlers were exercising the privilege of the franchise more than a year before Hooker preached his famous sermon declaring that the right of government lay in the people. There also is some reason to think that the leaders were still undecided whether or not to come to an agreement with the English lords and gentlemen and to put themselves under the latter's jurisdiction. But as Winthrop's commission expired at the end of a year and no new governor was appointed — the English Puritans having become absorbed in affairs at home — the Connecticut colony was thrown on its own resources and compelled to set up a government of its own. Pynchon at Springfield now cast in his lot with Massachusetts, and from this time forward Springfield was a part of the Massachusetts colony, but the men of Connecticut, disliking Pynchon's desertion, determined to act for themselves. On May 31, 1638, Hooker preached a sermon laying down the principles according to which government should be established; and during the six months that followed, the court, consisting of six magistrates and nine deputies, framed the Fundamental Orders, the laws that were to govern the colony.

This remarkable document, though deserving all the encomiums passed upon it, was not a constitution in any modern sense of the word and established nothing fundamentally new, because the form of government it outlined differed only in certain particulars from that of Massachusetts and Plymouth. It was made up of two parts, a preamble, which is a plantation covenant like that signed in the cabin of the *Mayflower*, and a series of laws or orders passed either separately or together by the court which drafted them. This court was a lawmaking body and it made public the laws when they were passed. That this body of laws or, as we may not improperly call it, this frame of government was ratified, as Trumbull says, by all the free planters assembled at Hartford on January 14, 1639, is not impossible, though such action would seem unnecessary as the court was a representative body, and unlikely as the time of year was not favorable for holding a mass-meeting at Hartford. Later courts never hesitated to change the articles without referring the changes to the planters. The articles simply confirmed the system of magistrates and deputies already in existence and added provisions for the election of a governor and deputy governor — who had not hitherto been chosen because of doubts regarding the jurisdiction of the English lords and gentlemen.

In matters of detail the Connecticut system

differed from that of Massachusetts in three
particulars: it imposed no religious test for those
entitled to vote, but required only that the
governor be a church member, though it is probable that in practice only those would be admitted
freemen who were covenanted Christians; it gave
less power to the magistrates and more to the
freemen; and it placed the election of the governor
in the hands of the voters, limiting their choice
only to a church member and a former magistrate,
and forbidding reëlection until after the expira-
tion of a year. Later the qualifications of a
freeman were made such that only about one in
every two or three voted in the seventeenth century; the powers of the magistrates were increased;
and the governor was allowed to succeed himself.
Connecticut was less democratic than Rhode
Island in the seventeenth century and, as the years
went on, fewer and fewer of the inhabitants exercised the freeman's privilege of voting for the
higher officials. By no stretch of the imagination
can the political conditions in any of the New England colonies be called popular or democratic.
Government was in the hands of a very few men.

Two more settlements remain to be considered
before a survey of the foundations of New England

can be called complete.   When the Reverend John
Wheelwright, the friend of Anne Hutchinson,
was driven from Massachusetts and took his way
northward to the region of Squamscott Falls
where he founded Exeter, he entered a territory
of grants and claims and rights of possession that
render the early history of New Hampshire a
tangle of difficulties.   Out of a grant to Gorges
and Mason of the stretch of coast between the
Merrimac and the Kennebec in 1622, and a confirmation of Mason's right to the region between
the Merrimac and the Piscataqua, arose the settlement of Strawberry Bank, or Portsmouth, and
accompanying it a controversy over the title to
the soil that lasted throughout the colonial period.
Mason called his territory New Hampshire;
Gorges planned to call the region that he received
New Somersetshire; and both designations took
root, one as the name of a colony, the other as
that of a county in Maine.   At an earlier date,
merchants of Bristol and Shrewsbury had become
interested in this part of New England and had
sent over one Edward Hilton, who some time
before 1627 began a settlement at Dover.   The
share of the Bristol merchants was purchased in
1633 by the English lords and gentlemen already

5

concerned in the Connecticut settlement, for the
purpose, it may be, of furnishing another refuge
in New England, should conditions at home demand their withdrawal overseas. But nothing
came of their purchase except an unfortunate
controversy with Plymouth colony over trading
boundaries on the Kennebec.

The men established on this northern frontier
were often lawless and difficult to control, of loose
habits and morals, and intent on their own profit;
and the region itself was inhospitable to organized
and settled government. Yet out of these somewhat nebulous beginnings, four settlements arose
— Portsmouth (Masonian and Anglican), Dover
(Anglican and Puritan), Exeter and Hampton
(both Puritan), each with its civil compact and
each an independent town. The inhabitants were
few in number, and "the generality, of mean
and low estates," and little disposed to union
among themselves. But in 1638–1639, when
Massachusetts discovered that one interpretation of her charter would carry her northern
boundary to a point above them, she took them
under her protecting wing. After considerable
debate this jurisdiction was recognized and the
New Hampshire and Maine towns were brought

within her boundaries. Henceforth, for many years a number of these towns, though in part Anglican communities and never burdened with the requirement that their freemen be church members, were represented in the general court at Boston. Nevertheless the Mason and Gorges adherents — whose Anglican and pro-monarchical sympathies were hostile to Puritan control and who were supported by the persistent efforts of the Mason family in England — were able to obtain the separation of New Hamsphire from Massachusetts in 1678. Maine, however, remained a part of the Bay Colony to the end of the colonial period.

The circumstances attending the settlement of New Haven were wholly unlike those of New Hampshire. John Davenport, a London clergyman of an extreme Puritan type, Theophilus Eaton, a London merchant in the Baltic trade and a member of the Eastland Company, Samuel Eaton and John Lathrop, two non-conforming ministers, were the leaders of the movement. Lathrop never went to New Haven, and Samuel Eaton early returned to England. The leaders and many of their followers were men of considerable property for that day, and their interest in trade gave to the colony a marked commercial character. The company was composed of men and women from London and its vicinity, and of others who joined them from Kent, Hereford, and Yorkshire. As both Davenport and Theophilus Eaton were members of the Massachusetts Bay Company, they were familiar with its work; and on coming to America in June, 1637, they stopped at Boston and remained there during the winter. Pressure was brought upon them to make Massachusetts their home, but without success, for though Davenport had much in common with the Massachusetts people, he was not content to remain where he would be merely one among many. Desiring a free place for worship and trade, he sent Eaton voyaging to find one; and the latter, who had heard of Quinnipiac on the Connecticut shore, viewed this spot and reported favorably. In March, 1638, the company set sail from Boston and laid the foundations of the town of New Haven.

This company had neither charter nor land grant, and, as far as we know, it had made no attempt to obtain either. "The first planters," says Kingsley, "recognized in their acts no human authority foreign to themselves." Unlike the Pilgrims in their *Mayflower* compact, they made no reference in their plantation covenant to the dread sovereign, King James, and in none of their acts and statements did they express a longing for their native country or regard for its authority. Their settlement bears some resemblance to that of the Rhode Island towns, but it was better organized and more orderly from the beginning. The settlers may have drawn up their covenant before leaving Boston and may have reached Quinnipiac as a community already united in a common civil and religious bond.   Their lands, which they purchased from the Indians, they laid out in their own way.   The next year on June 4, 1639, they held a meeting in Robert Newman's barn and there, declaring that the Word of God should be their guide in families and commonwealth and that only church members should be sharers in government, they chose twelve men as the foundations of their church state.   Two months later these twelve selected "seven pillars" who proceeded to organize a church by associating others with themselves.   Under the leadership of the seven the government continued until October, when they resigned and a gathering of the church members elected Theophilus Eaton as their magistrate and four others to act as assistants, with a secretary

and a treasurer. Thus was begun a form of
government which when perfected was very similar to that of the other New England colonies.

While New Haven as a town-colony was taking
on form, other plantations were arising near by.
Milford was settled partly from New Haven and
partly from Wethersfield, where an overplus of
clergy was leading to disputes and many with-
drawals to other parts. Guilford was settled directly from England. Southold on Long Island was
settled also from England, by way of New Haven.
Stamford had its origin in a Wethersfield quarrel,
when the Reverend Richard Denton, "blind of one
eye but not the least among the seers of Israel,"
departed with his flock. Branford also was
born of a Wethersfield controversy and later
received accessions from Long Island. In 1643,
Milford, Guilford, and Stamford combined under
the common jurisdiction of New Haven, to which
Southold and Branford acceded later with a form
of government copied after that of Massachusetts,
though the colony was distinctly federal in character, consisting of "the government of New Haven
with the plantations in combination therewith."
Though there was no special reservation of town
rights in the fundamental articles which defined

the government, yet the towns, five in number, considered themselves free to withdraw at any time if they so desired.

We have thus reviewed the conditions under which some forty towns, grouped under five jurisdictions, were founded in New England. They were destined to treble their number in the next generation and to suffer such regrouping as to reduce the jurisdictions to four before the end of the century — New Hampshire separating from Massachusetts, New Haven being absorbed by Connecticut, and Plymouth submitting to the authority of Massachusetts under the charter of 1691. In this readjustment we have the origin of four of the six New England States of the present day.

CHAPTER IV

EARLY NEW ENGLAND LIFE

THE people who inhabited these little New England towns were from nearly every grade of English society, but the greater number were men and women of humble birth — laborers, artisans, and petty farmers — drawn from town and country, possessed of scanty education, little or no financial capital, and but slight experience with the larger world. Some were middle-class lawyers, merchants, and squires; a few, but very few, were of higher rank, while scores were of the soil, coarse in language and habits, and given to practices characteristic of the peasantry of England at that time. The fact that hardly a fifth of those in Massachusetts were professed Christians renders it doubtful how far religious convictions were the only driving motive that sent hundreds of these men to New England. The leaders were, in a majority of cases, university men familiar with good literature and possessed of good libraries, but more cognizant of theology and philosophy than of the law and order of nature. Some were professional soldiers, simple in thought as they were courageous in action, while others were men of affairs, who had acquired experience before the courts and in the counting houses of England and were often amazingly versatile, able to turn their hands to any business that confronted them. For the great majority there was little opportunity in these early years to practice a trade or a profession. Except for the clergy, who could preach in America with greater freedom than in England, and for the occasional practitioner in physic or the law who as time went on found occasion to apply his knowledge in the household and the courts, there was little else for any one to do than engage in farming, fishing, and trading with the Indians, or turn carpenter and cobbler according to demand. The artisan became a farmer, though still preserving his knack as a craftsman, and expended his skill and his muscle in subduing a tough and unbroken soil.

New England was probably overstocked with men of strong minds and assertive dispositions. It was settled by radicals who would never have left the mother country had they not possessed well-formed opinions regarding some of the most important aspects of religious and social life. We may call them all Puritans, but as to the details of their Puritanism they often differed as widely as did Roundheads and Cavaliers in England. Though representative of a common movement, they were far from united in their beliefs or consistent in their political practices. There was always something of the inquisitor at Boston and of the monk at Plymouth, and in all the Puritan colonies there prevailed a self-satisfied sense of importance as the chosen of God. The controversies that arose over jurisdictions and boundaries and the niceties of doctrine are not edifying, however honest may have been those who entered into them. Massachusetts and Connecticut always showed a disposition to stretch their demands for territory to the utmost and to take what they could, sometimes with little charity or forbearance. The dominance of the church over the organization and methods of government and the rigid scrutiny of individual lives and habits, of which the leaders, notably those of Massachusetts, approved, were hardly in accord with democracy or personal liberty. Of toleration, except in Rhode Island, there was none.

The unit of New England life was the town, a self-governing community, in large measure complete in itself, and if left alone capable of maintaining a separate existence. Within certain limits, it was independent of higher authority, and in this respect it was unlike anything to be found in England. At this period, it was at bottom a religious community which owned and distributed the lands set apart for its occupation, elected its own officials, and passed local ordinances for its own well-being. At first, church members, landholders, and inhabitants tended to be identical, but they gradually separated as time went on and as new comers appeared and old residents migrated elsewhere. Before the end of the century, the ecclesiastical society, the board of land proprietors, and the town proper, even when largely composed of the same members, acted as separate groups, though the line of separation was often vague and was sometimes not drawn at all. Town meetings continued to be held in the meeting-house, and land was distributed by the town in its collective capacity. Lands were parceled out as they were needed in proportion to contributions to a common purchase fund or to family need, and later according to the ratable value of

a man's property. The fathers of Wallingford
in Connecticut, "considering that even single
persons industrious and laborious might through
the blessing of God increase and grow into families," distributed to the meanest bachelor "such
a quantity of land as might in an ordinary way
serve for the comfortable maintenance of a family."
Sometimes allotments were equal; often they
varied greatly in size, from an acre to fifty acres
and even more; but always they were determined
by a desire to be fair and just. The land was
granted in full right and could be sold or be-
queathed, though at first only with the consent
of the community. With the grant generally
went rights in woodland and pasture; and even
meadow land, after the hay was got in, was open
to the use of the villagers. The early New England town took into consideration the welfare and
contentment of the individual, but it rated as of
even greater importance the interests of the whole
body.

The settlements of New England inevitably presented great variations of local life and color,
stretching as they did from the Plymouth trucking posts in Maine, through the fishing villages of
Saco and York, and those on the Piscataqua, to the

towns of Long Island and the frontier communities of western Connecticut — Stamford and
Greenwich. The inhabitants to the number of
more than thirty thousand in 1640 were not only
in possession of the coast but were also pushing
their way into the interior. To fishing and agriculture they added trading, lumbering, and commerce, and were constantly reaching out for
new lands and wider opportunities. The Pilgrims had hardly weathered their first hard winter
when they rebuilt one of their shallops and sent
it northward on fishing and trading voyages;
and later they sent one bark up the Connecticut
and another to open up communication with the
Dutch at New Amsterdam. Pynchon was making Springfield the centre of the fur trade of the
interior, though an overcrowding of merchants
there was reducing profits and compelling the
settlers to resort to agriculture for a living. Of
all the colonies, New Haven was the most distinctly commercial. Stephen Goodyear built a
trucking house on an island below the great falls
of the Housatonic in 1642; other New Haven
colonists engaged in ventures on Delaware Bay;
and in 1645, the colony endeavored to open a
direct trade with England. But nearly every

New Haven enterprise failed, and by 1660 the
wealth of the colony had materially diminished
and the settlement had become "little else than
a colony of discouraged farmers." Among all the
colonies in New England and elsewhere there
was considerable coasting traffic, and vessels
went to Newfoundland and Bermuda, and even
to the distant West Indies, to Madeira, and to
Bilboa across the ocean. Ever since Winthrop
built the *Blessing of the Bay* in 1631, the first sea-
going craft launched in New England, Massachusetts had been the leading commercial colony,
and her vessels occasionally made the long tri-
angular voyage to Jamaica, and England, and
back to the Bay. The vessels carried planks, pipe
staves, furs, fish, and provisions, and exchanged
them for sugar, molasses, household goods, and
other wares and commodities needed for the
comfort and convenience of the colonists.

The older generation was passing away. By
1660, Winthrop, Cotton, Hooker, Haynes, Bradford, and Whiting were dead; Davenport and
Roger Williams were growing old; some of the
ablest men, Peters, Ludlow, Whitfield, Desborough,
Hooke, had returned to England, and others less
conspicuous had gone to the West Indies or to

the adjacent colonies. The younger men were coming on, new arrivals were creeping in, and a loosening of the old rigidity was affecting the social order. The Cambridge platform of 1648, which embodied the orthodox features of the Congregational system as determined up to that time, gave place to the Half-Way Covenant of 1657 and 1662, which owed its rise to the coming to maturity of the second generation, the children of the first settlers, now admitted to membership but not to full communion — a wide departure from the original purpose of the founders. Rhode Island continued to be the colony of separatism and soul liberty, where Seeker, Generalist, Anabaptist, and religious anarchist of the William Harris type found place, though not always peace. Cotton Mather later said there had never been "such a variety of religions together on so small a spot as there have been in that colony."

The coming of the Quakers to Boston in 1656, bringing with them as they did some of the very religious ideas that had caused Mrs. Hutchinson and John Wheelwright to be driven into exile, revived anew the old issue and roused the orthodox colonies to deny admission to ranters, heretics, Quakers, and the like. Boston burned their books as "corrupt, heretical, and blasphemous," flung these people into prison with every mark of indignity, branded them as enemies of the established order in church and commonwealth, and tried to prove that they were witches and emissaries of Satan. The first-comers were sent back to Barbados whence they came; the next were returned to England; those of 1657 were scourged; those of 1658, under the Massachusetts law of the previous year, were mutilated and, when all these measures had no effect, under the harsher law of October, 1658, four were hanged. One of these, Mary Dyer, though reprieved and banished, persisted in returning to her death. The Quakers were scourged in Plymouth, branded in New Haven, flogged at the cart's tail on Long Island, and chained to a wheelbarrow at New Amsterdam. Upon Connecticut they made almost no impression; only in Piscataqua, Rhode Island, Nantucket, and Eastern Long Island did they find a resting place.

To the awe inspired by the covenant with God was added the terror aroused by the dread power of Satan; and witchcraft inevitably took its place in the annals of New England Puritanism as it had done for a century in the annals of the

older world. Not one of the colonies, except
Rhode Island, was free from its manifestations.
Plymouth had two cases which came to trial, but
no executions; Connecticut and New Haven had
many trials and a number of executions, beginning with that of Alse Young in Windsor in 1647,
the first execution for witchcraft in New England.
The witch panic, a fearful exhibition of human
terror, appeared in Massachusetts as early as
1648, and ran its sinister course for more than
forty years, involving high and low alike and
disclosing an amazing amount of credulity and
superstition.   To the Puritan the power of Satan
was ever imminent, working through friend or
foe, and using the human form as an instrument
of injury to the chosen of God.   The great epidemic of witchcraft at Salem in 1692, the climax
and close of the delusion, resulted in the imprisonment of over two hundred persons and the execution of nineteen.   Some of those who sat in the
court of trial later came to their senses and were
heartily ashamed of their share in the proceedings.

The New Englander of the seventeenth century,
courageous as he was and loyal to his religious
convictions, was in a majority of cases gifted
with but a meager mental outfit.   The unknown

6

world frightened and appalled him; Satan warring with the righteous was an ever-present menace
to his soul; the will of God controlled the events
of his daily life, whether for good or ill. The
book of nature and the physiology and ailments
of his own body he comprehended with the mind
of a child. He believed that the planet upon
which he lived was the center of the universe,
that the stars were burning vapors, and the moon
and comets agencies controlling human destinies.
Strange portents presaged disaster or wrought
evil works. Many a New Englander's life was
governed according to the supposed influence of
the heavenly bodies; Bradford believed that there
was a connection between a cyclone and an eclipse;
and Morton defined an earthquake as a movement
of wind shut up in the pores and bowels of the
earth.

Of medicine the Puritans knew little and practised less. They swallowed doses of weird and
repelling concoctions, wore charms and amulets,
found comfort and relief in internal and external
remedies that could have had no possible influence upon the cause of the trouble, and when all
else failed they fell back upon the mercy and will
of God. Surgery was a matter of tooth-pulling

and bone-setting, and though post-mortems were
performed, we have no knowledge of the skill of
the practitioner.   The healing art, as well as nurs-
ing and midwifery, was frequently in the hands of
women, one of whom deposed: "I was able to
live by my chirurgery, but now I am blind and
cannot see a wound, much less dress it or make
salves"; and Jane Hawkins of Boston, the "bosom
friend" of Mrs. Hutchinson, was forbidden by the
general courts "to meddle in surgery or physic,
drink, plaisters or oils," as well as religion.   The
men who practised physic were generally home-
bred, making the greater part of their living at
farming or agriculture.   Some were ministers as
well as physicians, and one of them (Dr. Oliver
Wendell Holmes is sorry to say) "took to drink
and tumbled into the Connecticut River, and so
ended."   There were a number of regularly trained
doctors, such as John Clark of Newbury, Fuller
of Plymouth, Rossiter of Guilford, and others;
and the younger Winthrop, though not a physician,
had more than a smattering of medicine.

The mass of the New Englanders of the seventeenth century had but little education and but
few opportunities for travel.   As early as 1642,
Massachusetts required that every child should

be taught to read, and in 1647 enacted a law ordaining that every township should appoint a schoolmaster, and that the larger towns should each set up a grammar school. This well-known and much praised enactment, which made education the handmaid of religion and was designed to stem the tide of religious indifference rising over the colony, was better in intention than in execution. It had little effect at first, and even when under its provisions the common school gradually took root in New England, the education given was of a very primitive variety. Harvard College itself, chartered in 1636, was a seat of but a moderate amount of learning and at its best had only the training of the clergy in view. In Hartford and New Haven, grammar schools were founded under the bequest of Governor Hopkins, but came to little in the seventeenth century. In 1674, one Robert Bartlett left money for the setting up of a free school in New London, for the teaching of Latin to poor children, but the hope was richer than the fulfilment. In truth, of education for the laity at this time in New England there was scarcely more than the rudiments of reading, writing, and arithmetic. The frugal townspeople of New England generally deemed education an unnecessary expense; the school laws were evaded, and when complied with were more honored in the breach than in the observance. Even when honestly carried out, they produced but slender results. Probably most people could sign their names after a fashion, though many extant wills and depositions bear only the marks of their signers. Schoolmasters and town clerks had difficulties with spelling and grammar, and the rural population were too much engrossed by their farm labors to find much time for the improvement of the mind. Except in the homes of the clergy and the leading men of the larger towns there were few books, and those chiefly of a religious character. The English Bible and Bunyan's *Pilgrim's Progress*, printed in Boston in 1681, were most frequently read, and in the houses of the farmers the *British Almanac* was occasionally found. There were no newspapers, and printing had as yet made little progress.

The daily routine of clearing the soil, tilling the arable land, raising corn, rye, wheat, oats, and flax, of gathering iron ore from bogs and turpentine from pine trees, and in other ways of providing the means of existence, rendered life essentially stationary and isolated, and the mind was but slightly

quickened by association with the larger world.
A little journeying was done on foot, on horseback,
or by water, but the trip from colony to colony
was rarely undertaken; and even within the
colony itself but few went far beyond the borders
of their own townships, except those who sat as
deputies in the assembly or engaged in hunting,
trading, fishing, or in wars with the Indians. A
Connecticut man could speak of "going abroad"
to Rhode Island. Though in the larger towns
good houses were built, generally of wood and
sometimes of brick, in the remoter districts the
buildings were crude, with rooms on one floor and
a ladder to the chamber above, where corn was
frequently stored. Along the Pawcatuck River,
families lived in cellars along with their pigs.
Clapboards and shingles came in slowly as saw-
mills increased, but at first nails and glass were
rare luxuries. Conditions in such seaports as
Boston, where ships came and went and higher
standards of living prevailed, must not be taken
as typical of the whole country. The buildings of
Boston in 1683 were spoken of as "handsome, joining one to another as in London, with many large
streets, most of them paved with pebble stone."
Money in the country towns was merchantable

wheat, peas, pork, and beef at prices current.   Time
was reckoned by the farmers according to the sea-
sons, not according to the calendar, and men dated
events by "sweet corn time," "at the beginning of
last hog time," "since Indian harvest," and "the
latter part of seed time for winter wheat."

New England was a frontier land far removed
from the older civilizations, and its people were
always restive under restraint and convention.
They were in the main men and women of good
sense, sobriety, and thrift, who worked hard,
squandered nothing, feared God, and honored the
King, but the equipment they brought with them
to America was insufficient at best and had to
be replaced, as the years wore on, from resources
developed on New England soil.

CHAPTER V

AN ATTEMPT AT COLONIAL UNION

THE men who controlled the destinies of New England were deeply concerned not only with preserving its faith but also with guarding its rights and liberties as they defined them, and reverentially preserving the letter of its charters. For men who wished to sever their connection with England and to disregard English law and precedent as much as possible, they displayed a remarkable amount of respect for the documents that emanated from the British Chancery. In fact, however, they valued these grants and charters, not as expressions of royal favor, but as bulwarks against royal encroachment and outside interference, and in accepting such privileges as were conferred by their charters, they recognized no duty to be performed for the common mother, no obligations resting upon themselves to consider the welfare of England or to coöperate in her behalf.

The thoughts of these men were of themselves, their faith, and their problems of existence. The strongest ties were those that held together the people of a town, closely knit in the bond of a civil and religious covenant. Next above these were the ties of the colony, with its general court or assembly composed of representatives of the towns, its governor and other officials elected by the freemen, and its laws passed by the assembly for the benefit and well-being of all. Higher still was the loose bond of confederation that was fashioned in 1643 for the maintenance of order, peace, and security, in the form of a league of colonies. Highest, but weakest of all, was the bond that united them to England, recognized in sentiment but carrying with it no reciprocal obligations, either legal or otherwise. To the average inhabitant of New England, the mother country was merely the land from which he had come, the home to which he might or might not return. He had practically no knowledge of England's plans or policy, no comprehension of her purpose toward her colonies or the place of the colonies in her own scheme of expansion. He was absorbed in his own affairs, not in those of England; in the commands of God, not in those of the King; and in the dangers which surrounded him from the foes of the frontier, not in those which confronted England in her relations with her continental rivals. He was dominated by his instinct for self-government and by his compelling fear of the Stuarts and all that they represented. Even during the period of the Commonwealth and the Protectorate, England was three thousand miles away, appeal to her was difficult and costly, and the English brethren were not always as sympathetic as they might have been with the aims and methods of their co-religionists.

This very isolation from the mother country, at a time when the New Englanders were pushing their fur-trading activities into the regions claimed by the Dutch and the French, rendered some sort of united action necessary and desirable. The settlers were of one stock and one purpose. Despite bickerings and disputes, they shared a common desire to enjoy the liberties of the Christian religion and to obtain from the new country into which they had come both subsistence and profit. The determination to open up trading posts on the Penobscot, the Delaware, and the Hudson, and to utilize all waters for their fisheries brought them into conflict with their rivals, at New Am-

sterdam and in Nova Scotia, and made it imperative, should any one colony — Plymouth,
Massachusetts, Connecticut, or New Haven —
attempt to pursue its plans alone, for all to band
together in its support.   The troubles already en-
countered with the Dutch on the Delaware and the
Connecticut and with the French in Maine, in the
competition for the fur trade of the interior, had
rendered the situation acute and led, very early,
to the proposal that a combination be effected.

But it was not until 1643 that anything was
accomplished. In May of that year, at the
suggestion of Connecticut and New Haven, commissioners from these colonies, and from Massachusetts and Plymouth also, met at Boston and
drafted a body of articles for a consociation or
confederation to be known as the United Colonies
of New England, a form of union which found a
precedent in the federation of the Netherlands
and corresponded in the political field to the consociation of churches in the ecclesiastical. Maine
was not asked because, as a province belonging
to Gorges, the people there (to quote from Winthrop's *Journal*) "ran a different course from the
other colonies, both in their ministry and civil
administration, . . . had lately made Acomenti-

cus (a poor village) a corporation, and had made a taylor their mayor, and had entertained one Hull, an excommunicated person and very contentious, for their minister." Rhode Island, as a seat of separatism and heresy, was not invited and perhaps not even considered. For managing the affairs of the confederation, the main objects of which were friendship and amity, protection and defense, advice and succor, and the preservation of the truth and purity of the Gospel, eight commissioners were provided, to be chosen by the assemblies of the colonies and to represent the colonies as independent political units. Meetings were to be held once a year in one or other of the leading towns and a full record was to be kept of the business done. The board thus established never did more than make recommendations and offer advice, as it had no authority to execute any of the plans that it might make; and although the records of its meetings are lengthy and give evidence of elaborate discussion of important matters, the results of its deliberations cannot be said to be particularly significant.

The commissioners dealt with a number of local disputes of no great moment and considered certain internal difficulties that threatened to disturb the friendly intercourse among the colonies. For instance, Connecticut had levied tolls at Saybrook on vessels going up the Connecticut River to Springfield, and Massachusetts had retaliated by laying duties on goods from other colonies entering her ports. Under pressure from the commissioners both the colonies receded from their positions. Again, the commissioners recommended the granting of aid to Harvard College, and that institution consequently received from Connecticut and New Haven annually for many years a regular allowance, in return for which it presented the Connecticut colony with nearly sixty graduates in the ensuing half-century well equipped to combat latitudinarianism and heresy. The commissioners fulfilled their obligation as guardians of the purity of the Gospel, both in their support of the synod of 1646–1648 and in their strenuous efforts to check the increase of religious discontent due to the narrow definition of church membership — efforts which eventually resulted in that "illogical compromise," the Half-Way Covenant. They recommended the driving out of "Quakers, Ranters, and other Herritics of that nature," and urged that the true Gospel might be spread among the Indians. They up-

held the work of the Society for the Promoting
and Propagating of the Gospel of Jesus Christ
in New England, and they directed and guided
the labors of its missionaries, most notable of
whom was the famous John Eliot, apostle to the
Indians and translator of the Bible into their
language.

The most important business of the confederation concerned the defense of New England against
the Indians, the Dutch, and the French. The
Indians were an ever-present menace, near and
far; the Dutch disputed the English claims all
the way from New Amsterdam to Narragansett
Bay, and resented the attempts already made to
encroach upon their trading grounds; and the
French at this time were strenuously denying the
right of the English, particularly those of Plymouth, to establish trading-posts at Machias and
on the Penobscot, and were laying claim to all
the Nova Scotian territory as far west as the
Penobscot.

Though the French, in their effort to drive out
all the English settlers east of Pemaquid in Maine,
had destroyed two Plymouth posts in that region,
the commissioners were called upon to decide
not so much what should be done about this act

of aggression, as which of the claimants among
the French themselves it was wiser for the colonies
to support.   A certain Charles de la Tour had
been commissioned by the Governor-General of
Acadia or Nova Scotia as lieutenant of the region
east of the St. Croix, and another, Charles de
Menou, Sieur d'Aulnay-Charnisé, as lieutenant of
the region between the St. Croix and the Penobscot.   When the Governor-General died in 1635,
a contest for the governorship took place between
these two men, and not unnaturally volunteers
from Massachusetts aided La Tour, whose original
jurisdiction was farthest removed from their
colony.   Trade on these northeastern coasts was
deemed essential to the prosperity of the New
Englanders, and it was considered of great importance to make no mistake in backing the wrong
claimant.   D'Aulnay, or more correctly Aulnay,
had been partly responsible for the attack on the
Plymouth trading-posts, but, on the other hand,
he had the stronger title; and Massachusetts was
a good deal perplexed as to what course to pursue.   In 1644, Aulnay sent a commissioner to
Boston, who conversed with Governor Endecott
in French and with the rest of the magistrates in
Latin and endeavored to arrange terms of peace.

Two years later the same commissioner came again, with two others, and was cordially entertained with "wine and sweetmeats." The matter was referred to the commissioners of the United Colonies, who decided, with considerable shrewdness, that the volunteers in aiding La Tour had acted efficiently but not wisely; and consequently a compromise was reached. Aulnay's commissioners abated their claims for damages, and Governor Winthrop consented to send "a small present" to Aulnay in lieu of compensation. The present was "a fair new sedan (worth," says Winthrop, "forty or fifty pounds, where it was made, but of no use to us)," having been part of some Spanish booty taken in the West Indies and presented to the Governor. So final peace was made at no expense to the colony; and later, after Aulnay's death in 1650, La Tour married the widow and came to his own in Nova Scotia.

The troubles with the Dutch were not so easily settled. England had never acknowledged the Dutch claim to New Amsterdam, and the New England Council in making its grants had paid no attention to the Dutch occupation. Though trade had been carried on and early relations had

been on the whole amicable, yet, after Connecticut's overthrow of the Pequots in 1637 and the opening of the territory to settlement, the founding of towns as far west as Stamford and Greenwich had rendered acute the conflict of titles. There was no western limit to the English claims, and, as the colonists were perfectly willing to accept Sir William Boswell's advice to "crowd on, crowding the Dutch out of those places which they have occupied, without hostility or any act of violence," a collision was bound to come. The Dutch, who in their turn were not abating a jot of their claims, had already destroyed a New Haven settlement on the Delaware, and had asserted rights of jurisdiction even in New Haven harbor, by seizing there one of their own ships charged with evading the laws of New Amsterdam. Peter Stuyvesant, the Dutch Governor, famous for his short temper and mythical silver leg, visited Hartford in 1650, and negotiated with the commissioners of the United Colonies a treaty drawing the boundary line from the west side of Greenwich Bay northward twenty miles. But this treaty, though ratified by the States General of Holland, was never ratified by England, and, when two years later war between the two coun-

tries broke out overseas, the question of an
attack on New Amsterdam was taken up and
debated with such heat as nearly to disrupt the
Confederation. The absolute refusal of Massachusetts to enter on such an undertaking so prolonged the discussion that the war was over before
a decision was reached; but Connecticut seized
the Dutch lands at Hartford, and Roger Ludlow,
who had moved to Fairfield from Windsor after
1640, began an abortive military campaign of his
own. The situation remained unchanged as long
as the Dutch held New Netherland, and the region
between Greenwich and the Bronx continued to
be what it had been from the beginning of settlement, a territory occupied only by Indians and a
few straggling emigrants. There the unfortunate
Anne Hutchinson with her family was massacred
by the Indians in 1643.

The New England Confederation performed
the most important part of its work during the
first twenty years of its existence, for although it
lasted nominally till 1684, it ceased to be effective
after 1664, and was of little weight in New England history after the restoration of the Stuarts.
Owing to the fact that it had been formed without any authority from England, the Confederation

was never recognized by the Government there, and with the return of the monarchy it survived chiefly as an occasional committee meeting for debate and advice.

CHAPTER VI

WINNING THE CHARTERS

THE accession of Charles II to the throne of England provoked a crisis in the affairs of the Puritans and gave rise to many problems that the New Englanders had not anticipated and did not know how to solve. With a Stuart again in control, there were many questions that might be easily asked but less easily answered. Except for Massachusetts and Plymouth, not a settlement had a legal title to its soil; and except for Massachusetts, not one had ever received a sufficient warrant for the government which it had set up. Naturally, therefore, there was disquietude in Rhode Island, Connecticut, and New Haven; and even Massachusetts, buttressed as she was, feared lest the King might object to many of the things she had done. Entrenched behind her charter and aware of her superiority in wealth, territory, and population, she had taken the leader-

ship in New England and had used her opportunity to intimidate her neighbors. Except for
New Haven, not a colony or group of settlements
but had felt the weight of her claims. Plymouth
and Connecticut had protested against her demands; the Narragansett towns with difficulty
had evaded her attempt to absorb them; and the
settlements at Piscataqua and on the Maine coast
had finally yielded to her jurisdiction. As long
as Cromwell lived and the Government of England
was under Puritan direction, Massachusetts had
little to fear from protests against her; but, with
the Cromwellian régime at an end, she could not
expect from the restored monarchy a favoring or
friendly attitude.

The change in England was not merely one of
government; it was one of policy as well. Even
during the Cromwellian period, Englishmen awoke
to a greater appreciation of the importance of
colonies as assets of the mother country, and
began to realize, in a fashion unknown to the
earlier period, the necessity of extending and
strengthening England's possessions in America.
England was engaged in a desperate commercial
war with Holland, whose vessels had obtained a
monopoly of the carrying trade of the world; and

to win in that conflict it was imperative that her statesmen should husband every resource that the kingdom possessed. The religious agitations of previous years were passing away and the New England colonies were not likely to be troubled on account of their Puritanism. The great question in England was not religious conformity but national strength based on commercial prosperity.

Thus England was fashioning a new system and defining a new policy. By means of navigation acts, she barred the Dutch from the carrying trade and confined colonial commerce in large part to the mother country. She established councils and committees of trade and plantations, and, by the seizure of New Netherland in 1664 and the grant of the Carolinas and the Bahamas in 1663 and 1670, she completed the chain of her possessions in America from New England to Barbados. A far-flung colonial world was gradually taking shape, demanding of the King and his advisers an interest in America of a kind hitherto unknown. It is not surprising that so vast a problem, involving the trade and defense of nearly twenty colonies, should have made the internal affairs of New England seem of less consequence to the royal authorities than had been the case in the days of Charles I and Archbishop Laud, when the obtaining of the Massachusetts Bay charter had roused such intensity of feeling in England. What was interesting Englishmen was no longer the matter of religious obedience in the colonies, but rather that of their political and commercial dependence on the mother country.

As the future of New England was certain to be debated at Whitehall after 1660, the colonies took pains to have representatives on the ground to meet criticisms and complaints, to ward off attacks, and to beg for favors. Rhode Island sent a commission to Dr. John Clarke, one of her founders and leading men, at that time in London, instructing him to ask for royal protection, self-government, liberty of conscience, and a charter. Massachusetts sent Simon Bradstreet and the Reverend John Norton, with a petition that reads like a sermon, praying the King not to listen to other men's words but to grant the colonists an opportunity to answer for themselves, they being "true men, fearers of God and the King, not given to change, orthodox and peaceable in Israel." Connecticut, with more worldly wisdom, sent John Winthrop, the Governor, a man courtly and tactful, with a petition shrewdly worded and to the point. Plymouth entrusted her mission also to Winthrop, hoping for a confirmation of her political and religious liberties. All protested their loyalty to the Crown, while Massachusetts, her petition signed by the stiff-necked Endecott, prostrated herself at the royal feet, craving pardon for her boldness, and subscribing herself "Your Majesties most humble subjects and suppliants." Did Endecott remember, we wonder, a certain incident connected with the royal ensign at Salem?

Against the lesser colonies no complaints were presented, except in the case of New Haven, which was charged by the inhabitants of Shelter Island with usurpation of their goods and territory; but for Massachusetts the restoration of the Stuarts opened a veritable Pandora's box of troubles. In "divers complaints, petitions, and other informations concerning New England," she was accused of overbearance and oppression, of seizing the territory of New Hampshire and Maine, of denying the rights of Englishmen to Anglicans and non-freemen of the colony, and of persecuting the Quakers and others of religious views different from her own. She was declared to be seeking independence of Crown and Parliament by forbidding appeals to England, refusing to enforce the oath of allegiance to the King, and in general exceeding the powers laid down in her charter. The new plantations council, commissioned by the King in December, 1660, sent a peremptory letter the following April ordering the colony to proclaim the King "in the most solemn manner," and to hold herself in readiness to answer complaints by appointing persons well instructed to represent her before itself in England. At the same time, it begged the King to go slowly, giving Massachusetts an opportunity to be heard, and to write a letter "with all possible tenderness," pointing out that submission to the royal authority was absolutely essential. This the King did, confirming the charter of Massachusetts, renewing the colony's rights and privileges, and in conciliatory fashion ascribing all derelictions of duty to the iniquity of the times rather than to any evil intention of the heart. Then declaring that the chief aim of the charter was liberty of conscience, the King struck at the very heart of the Massachusetts system, by commanding the magistrates to grant full liberty of worship to members of the Anglican Church and the right to vote to all who were "orthodox" in religion and possessed of "competent estates." Though this order was evaded by various definitions of "orthodox" and "competent estates" and was not to be fully executed for many years, yet its meaning was clear — no single religious body would ever again be allowed, by the royal authorities in England, to monopolize the government or control the political destinies of a British colony in America or elsewhere.

The policy thus adopted toward Massachusetts became even more conciliatory when applied to the other colonies. It is not improbable that the King's advisers saw in the strengthening of Connecticut and Rhode Island an opportunity to check the power of Massachusetts and to reduce her importance in New England. However that may be, they lent themselves to the efforts that Winthrop and Clarke were making to obtain charters for their respective colonies. These agents were able, discreet, and broadminded men. Clarke, a resident in England for a number of years, had acquired no little personal influence; and Winthrop, as an old-time friend of the English lords and gentlemen whose governor he had been at Saybrook, could count on the help of the one surviving member of that group, Lord Saye and Sele, who was a privy councillor, a member of the

House of Lords and of the plantations council, and, as we are told, Lord Privy Seal, a position that would be of direct service in expediting the issue of a charter. Winthrop had personal qualities, also, that made for success. He was a university man, had made the grand tour of the Continent, and was familiar with official traditions and the ways of the court. Soon after his arrival in England, he became a member of the Royal Society and served on several of its committees, and thus had an opportunity of making friends and of showing his interest in other things than theology. If Cotton Mather was rightly informed, Winthrop was accorded a personal interview with Charles II and presented the King with a ring which Charles I, as Prince of Wales, had given his grandfather, Adam Winthrop.

Winthrop made good use of a good cause. Connecticut had behaved herself well and had incurred no ill-will. She had had no dealings with the Cromwellian Government, had dutifully proclaimed the King, had been discreet in her attitude toward Whalley and Goffe, the regicides who had fled to New England, and had aroused no resentment against herself among her neighbors. With proceedings once begun, the securing of the charter

went rapidly forward. Winthrop at first peti-
tioned for a confirmation of the old Warwick
patent, which had been purchased of the English
lords and gentlemen in 1644, but later, encouraged
it may be by friends in England, he asked for a
charter. The request was granted.[1] The document gave to Connecticut the same boundaries
as those of the old patent, and conferred powers
of government identical with those of the Fundamental Orders of 1639. That the main features
of the charter were drawn up in the colony before
Winthrop sailed is probable, though it is not
impossible that they were drafted in London by
Winthrop himself. All that the English officials
did was to give the text its proper legal form.

After the receipt of the charter and its proclamation in the colony and after a slight readjustment
of the government to meet the few changes required, the general court of Connecticut proceeded to enforce the full territorial rights of the
colony. The men of Connecticut had made up
their minds, now that the charter had come, to
execute its terms to the uttermost and to extend
the authority of the colony to the farthest bounds,

[1] The King's warrant was issued on February 28, the writ of
Privy Seal on April 23, and the great seal was affixed on May 10,
1662.

so that, next to the government of the Bay, Connecticut might be the greatest in New England. The court took under its protection the towns of Stamford and Greenwich, and on the ground that the whole territory westward was within its jurisdiction warned the Dutch governor not to meddle. It accepted the petition of Southold on Long Island and of certain residents of Guilford, both of the New Haven federation, for annexation, and, sending a force to Long Island to demand the surrender of the western towns there, it seized Captain John Scott, who was planning to establish a separate government over them, and brought him to Hartford for trial. It informed the towns of Mystic and Pawcatuck, lying in the disputed land between Connecticut and Rhode Island, that they were in the Connecticut colony and must henceforth conduct their affairs according to its laws. The relations with Rhode Island were to be a matter of later adjustment, and no immediate trouble followed; but Stuyvesant, the Dutch Governor, protested angrily against Connecticut's claim to Dutch territory and brought the matter to the attention of the commissioners of the United Colonies. On one pretext or another, the latter delayed action; and the matter was not settled until England's seizure of New Amsterdam in 1664 brought the Dutch rule to an end and made operative the royal grant of the territory to the Duke of York, thus stopping Connecticut in her somewhat headlong career westward and taking from her the whole of Long Island and all the land west of the Connecticut River. If maintained, this grant would have reduced the colony by half and would have materially retarded its progress; but Connecticut eventually saved the western portion of her territory as far as the line of 1650. However, her people could do no more crowding on into the region beyond, for the province of New York now lay directly across the path of her westward expansion.

But with New Haven her success was complete. That unfortunate colony, which had made an effort to obtain a patent in 1645, when the "great ship," bearing the agent Gregson, had foundered with all on board, had no friends at court, and had been too poor after 1660 to join the other colonies in sending an agent to London. Consequently its right to exist as an independent government was not considered in the negotiations which Winthrop had carried on. Serious complaints had been raised against it; its rigorous theocratic policy had created divisions among its own people, many of whom had begun to protest; it had been friendly with the Cromwellian régime and had proclaimed Charles II unwillingly and after long delay; it had protected the regicides until the messengers sent out for their capture could report the colony as "obstinate and pertinacious in contempt of His Majestie." Governor Leete, of the younger generation, was not in sympathy with Davenport's persistent refusal of all overtures from Hartford, and would probably have favored union under the charter of 1662 if Connecticut had been less aggressive in her attitude. As it was, the controversy became pungent and was prolonged for more than two years, though the outcome was never uncertain. The New Haven colony was poor, unprotected, and divided against itself. Its population was decreasing; Indian massacres threatened its frontiers; the malcontents of Guilford, led by Bray Rossiter, were demanding immediate and unconditional surrender to Connecticut; and finally in 1664 the successful capture of New Netherland and the grant to the Duke of York threatened the colony with annexation from that quarter. Rather than be joined to New York, New Haven surrendered.

One by one the towns broke away until in December
of that year only Branford, Guilford, and New
Haven remained. On December 13, 1664, the
freemen of these towns, with a few others, voted
to submit, "as from a necessity . . . but with a
salvo jure of our former right & claime, as a
people who have not yet been heard in point of
plea."

The New Haven federation was dissolved;
Davenport withdrew to Boston, where he became
a participant in the religious life of that colony;
and the strict Puritans of Branford, Guilford, and
Milford, led by Abraham Pierson, went to New
Jersey and founded Newark. The towns, left
loose and at large, joined Connecticut voluntarily
and separately, and the New Haven colony ceased
to exist. But the dual capital of Connecticut and
the alternate meetings of its legislature in Hartford and New Haven, marked for more than two
hundred years the twofold origin of the colony
and the state.

In the meantime Rhode Island had become a
legally incorporated colony. Even before Winthrop sailed for England, Dr. John Clarke had
received a favorable reply to his petition for a
charter. But a year passed and nothing was done

about the matter, probably owing to the arrival of
Winthrop and the feeling of uncertainty aroused by
the conflicting boundary claims, which involved
a stretch of some twenty-five miles of territory
between Narragansett Bay and the Pawcatuck
River. A third claimant also appeared, the Ather-
ton Company, with its headquarters in Boston,
which had purchased lands of the Indians at
various points in the area and held them under
the jurisdiction of Massachusetts. When Clarke
heard that Winthrop, in drawing the boundaries for the Connecticut charter of 1662, had included this Narragansett territory, he protested
vehemently to the King, saying that Connecticut had "injuriously swallowed up the one-half
of our colonie," and demanding a reconsidera-
tion. Finally, after the question had been debated in the presence of Clarendon and others,
the decision was reached to give Rhode Island the
boundaries and charter she desired, but to leave
the question of conflicting claims for later settlement. Evidently Winthrop, though not agreeing
with Clarke in matters of fact regarding the boundaries, supported Rhode Island's appeal for a
charter, for Clarendon said afterwards that the
draft which Clarke presented had in it expressions

8

that were disliked, but that the charter was granted out of regard for Winthrop.

The Rhode Island charter passed the seals July 8, 1663, and was received in the colony four months later with great joy and thanksgiving. It created a common government for all the towns, guaranteeing full liberty "in religious concernments" and freedom from all obligations to conform to the "litturgy, formes, and ceremonyes of the Church of England, or take or subscribe the oathes and articles made and established in that behalfe." This may have been the phrase that Clarendon, who was a High Churchman, objected to when the draft was presented. The form of government was similar in all essential particulars to that of Connecticut.

Rhode Island's enthusiasm in obtaining a charter is not difficult to understand. That amphibious colony, consisting of mainland, islands, and a large body of water, was inhabited by "poor despised peasants," as Governor Brenton described them, "living remote in the woods" and subject to the "envious and subtle contrivances of our neighbour colonies round about us, who are in a combination united together to swallow us up." The colony had not been asked to join the New

England Confederation, and its leaders were convinced that the members of the Confederation were in league to filch away their lands and, by driving them into the sea, to eliminate the colony altogether. Plymouth, seeking a better harbor than that of Plymouth Bay, claimed the eastern mainland as well as the chief islands, Hog, Conanicut, and Aquidneck; Massachusetts claimed Pawtuxet, Warwick, and the Narragansett country generally; while Connecticut wished to push her eastern boundary as far beyond the Pawcatuck River (the present boundary) as she might be able to do. Had each of these colonies made good its claim, there would have been little left of Rhode Island, and we do not wonder that the settlers looked upon themselves as fighting, with their backs to the sea, for their very existence. Hence they welcomed the charter with the joy of one relieved of a great burden, for, though the boundary question remained unsettled, the charter assured the colony of its right to exist under royal protection.

CHAPTER VII

MASSACHUSETTS DEFIANT

MASSACHUSETTS was yet to be taken in hand.
The English authorities had become convinced
that a satisfactory settlement of all the difficulties in New England could be undertaken not in
England, where the facts were hard to get at, but
in America. Lord Clarendon, the Chancellor, had
been in correspondence with Samuel Maverick,
an early settler in New England and for many
years a resident of Boston and New Amsterdam.
As an Anglican, Maverick had sympathized with
the opposition in Massachusetts led by Dr.
Robert Child, and had been debarred from all
civil and religious rights in the colony; but he
was a man of sobriety and good judgment, whose
chief cause of offense was a difference of opinion
as to how a colony should conduct its government.
The fact that he had been able to get on with the
Massachusetts men shows that his attitude had

never been seriously aggressive, for though he certainly had no liking for the policy of the colony, he does not appear to have been influenced by any hostility towards Massachusetts.

Happening to be in England at this juncture, Maverick was called upon by the Chancellor to state the case against the colony, and this he did in several letters, giving many instances of the colony's disloyalty and injustice, and recommending that its privileges be taken away, just as it had taken away the privileges of others. To this suggestion Clarendon paid no heed, for it was no part of the royal purpose to drive the colonies to desperation at a time when the King was but newly come to his throne and needed all his resources in the struggle with the Dutch. But to Maverick's further suggestions that New Netherland be reduced, that Massachusetts be regulated, and that commissioners be sent over to accomplish these ends, he expressed himself as favorable, and all were finally accepted by the Government. Maverick's opinion that British control should be exercised over a British possession and that the government of such a possession should not be conducted after the fashion of an ecclesiastical society happened to coincide with that of the

King's advisers and, as Maverick had lived in America for thirty years, his advice was listened to with respect and approval. All thought that, while Massachusetts might not be driven with safety, she could probably be persuaded to admit some alteration in her methods of government by tactful representatives.

Had the Duke of York, to whom was entrusted the task of selecting the new commissioners, chosen his men as wisely as Clarendon had shaped his policy, the results, as far as Massachusetts was concerned, might have been more successful. The trouble lay with the character of the work to be done. On the one hand the Dutch colony was to be seized by force of arms, a military undertaking involving boldness and executive ability; on the other, the Puritan colonies were to be regulated, a mission which called for the utmost tact. The men chosen for the work were far from the best that might have been selected to bring back to the path of true obedience and impartial justice a colony that was deemed wilful and perverse. They were Richard Nicolls, a favorite of the Duke of York and the only commissioner possessed of discrimination and wisdom, but who, as governor of the yet unconquered

Dutch colony, was likely to be taken up with his duties to such an extent as to preclude his sharing prominently in the diplomatic part of his mission; Colonel George Cartwright, a soldier, well-meaning but devoid of sympathy and ignorant of the conditions that confronted him; Sir Robert Carr, the worst of the four, unprincipled and profligate and without control either of his temper or his passions; and, lastly, Maverick himself, opposed to the existing order in Massachusetts and convinced of the necessity of radical changes in the constitution of the colony. Nicolls was liked and respected; Cartwright and Carr were distrusted as soldiers and strangers, and their presence was resented; whereas Maverick was objected to as a malcontent who had gone to England to complain and had returned with power to make trouble. When the colony heard of his appointment, it sent a vigorous address of protest to the King. If Clarendon expected from the last three of these men the wisdom and discretion that he said were essential to the task, he strangely misjudged their characters. He thought, to be sure, of adding other commissioners from New England, but he did not know whom to select and was fearful of arousing local jealousies. Yet considering the work to be done, it is doubtful if any commissioners, no matter how wisely selected, could have performed the task, for Massachusetts did not want to be regulated.

The general object of the commission was "to unite and reconcile persons of very different judgments and practice in all things," particularly concerning "the peace and prosperity of the people and their joint submission and obedience to us and our government." More specifically, the commissioners were to effect the overthrow of the Dutch, investigate conditions among the Indians, capture the regicides, secure obedience to the navigation acts, look into the question of boundaries, and determine the title to the Narragansett country, henceforth to be called the King's Province. The commissioners were to make it clear that they were not come to interfere with the prevailing religious systems, but to demand liberty of conscience for all, though Clarendon could not repress the hope that ultimately the New Englanders might return to the Anglican fold. The secret instructions were even more remarkable as evidence of a complete misunderstanding of conditions in New England. Clarendon wished to secure for the Crown the power to

nominate or at least to approve the governor of
Massachusetts, to control the militia, and to
examine and correct the laws — powers, it may be
noted, which were exercised in every royal colony
as a matter of course. He suggested that the
commissioners interest themselves in the elections so far as "to gett men of the best reputa-
tion and most peaceably inclined" chosen to the
assembly, but he cautioned them to "proceed
very warily" in some of these things. He had a
hope that Massachusetts might be so wrought
upon as to choose Nicolls for her governor and
Carr for her major-general, but in this, as in
the pious hope of a return of the Puritans to
the Church of England, he reckoned without a
knowledge of the grimness of the Massachusetts
temper.

The commissioners reached Boston, *en route* for
New Amsterdam, late in July, 1664, asked for
troops, and demanded the repeal of the franchise
law. The magistrates took the precaution to
conceal the charter; they were also heartily glad
when the commissioners departed on their errand
of conquest and hoped they would not return.
The general court, having modified the franchise
law sufficiently to meet the letter of the King's

command, wrote His Majesty that they wished he would recall his emissaries; and when the magistrates discovered that this impertinent demand not only failed of its object but drew down upon the colony a royal rebuke, with characteristic shrewdness they shifted their ground and prepared to meet the commissioners in fair contest, wearing out their patience and thwarting their plans by every available device. In the meantime, the four men were completing the conquest and pacification of New Netherland, and rearranging the boundary difficulties with Connecticut. Then Maverick and Cartwright passed on to Boston, where they were joined in February by Carr, Nicolls remaining in New York. The three men, making Boston their headquarters, visited Plymouth, Newport, and Hartford, where they were received, according to their account, "with great expressions of loyalty" — a statement which, if true, shows how successfully the colonists suppressed their deeper feelings. Having taken the King's Province under the royal protection, and postponed for later consideration the question of the boundary line between Rhode Island and Connecticut, with new complaints against Massachusetts ringing in their ears, they returned to Boston to meet the defiant magistrates. There Nicolls joined them in May.

The Massachusetts mission was hopeless from the beginning. The magistrates and general court would not admit the right of the commissioners to interfere in any way with governmental procedure or with the course of justice; and standing with absolute firmness on the powers granted by the charter and pointing to the recent renewal by the King as a full confirmation of all their privileges, they denied the validity of the royal mission and refused to discuss the question of jurisdiction. The commissioners said very plainly that Massachusetts had not administered the oath of allegiance or permitted the use of the Book of Common Prayer, as she had promised to do, and, as for the new franchise law, they did not understand it themselves and did not believe it would meet the royal requirements. To none of these points did the magistrates make any sufficient reply, but, feeling convinced that safety lay in avoiding decisions, they preferred rather to leave the matter ambiguous than to attempt any clearing up of the points at issue.

But when the commissioners took up the question of appeals and announced their determina-

tion to sit as a court of justice, the issue was more
fairly joined. The magistrates quoted the text
of the charter to show that the colony had full
power over all judicial affairs, while the commissioners cited their instructions as a sufficient
warrant for their right to hear complaints against
the colony. A deadlock ensued, but in the end
the colony triumphed. After spending a month
in fruitless negotiations, the commissioners gave
up the struggle, preferring to leave the conduct
of Massachusetts to be passed upon by the Crown
rather than to prolong the controversy. For the
time being, the Massachusetts men had their
own way; but they had raised a serious and dangerous question, that of their allegiance and its
obligations, for, as the commissioners said, "The
King did not grant away his soveraigntie over
you when he made you a corporation. When
His Majestie gave you power to make wholesome
lawes and to administer justice, he parted not
with his right of judging whether those laws are
wholsom, or whether justice was administered
accordingly or no. When His Majestie gave you
authoritie over such of his subjects as lived within
the limits of your jurisdiction, he made them not
your subjects nor you their supream authority."

Had the magistrates been wiser men, less home-bred and provincial, and possessed of wider vision, they would have foreseen the dangers that confronted them. But Bellingham and Leverett, the leading representatives of the policy of no surrender, were not men gifted with foresight, and they remained unmoved by the last threat of the commissioners that it would be hazardous to deny the King's supremacy, for " 'tis possible that the charter which you so much idolize may be forfeited."

The magistrates were undoubtedly influenced by the character of the commissioners and their rough and ready methods of procedure. Had all been as honorable and upright as Nicolls, who unfortunately took but little part in the negotiations, the outcome might have been different. But there is reason to think otherwise. The Massachusetts leaders took the ground that if they yielded any part they must eventually yield all, and they wanted no interference from outside in their government. Having ruled themselves for thirty years as they thought best, they were not disposed to admit that the King had any rights in the colony; and they believed that by steady resistance or by dilatory practices they could stave off intervention and that, with the danger once removed, the colony would be allowed to continue in its own course. In a measure they were justified in their belief. The King recalled the commissioners, and, though he wrote a letter declaring that Massachusetts had shown a great want of duty and respect for the royal authority, he went no further than to command the colony to send agents to England to answer there the questions that had not been settled during the stay of the commissioners at Boston. But the colony did not take this command seriously and sent no agents. Nicolls, always temperate in speech, wrote in 1666: "The grandees of Boston are too proud to be dealt with, saying that His Majesty is well satisfied with their loyalty."

The "grandees" were playing a shrewd but none too wise a game. Affairs in England were not favorable to the pursuit of a rigorous policy at this time. The Dutch war, the fire and epidemic in London, and the consequent suspension of all outside activities, had thrown governmental business into disorder and confusion. Clarendon, whose influence was waning, was soon to lose his post as Chancellor. The negotiations which ended in the treaty of Breda, and the threatening policy of Louis XIV, now beginning to take a form ominous to the Protestant states of Europe, distracted men's minds at home, and the Massachusetts problem was for the moment lost sight of in the presence of the larger issues. The colony returned to its former position of independence and soon reasserted its former authority over New Hampshire and Maine. To all appearances the failure of the royal commissioners was complete, but appearances were deceptive. The issue lay not merely between a Stuart King and a colony seeking to preserve its liberties; it was part of the larger and more fundamental issue of the place of a colony in England's newly developed policy of colonial subordination and control. Neither was Massachusetts a persecuted democracy. No modern democratic state would ever vest such powers in the hands of its magistrates and clergy, nor would any modern people accept such oppressive and unjust legislation as characterized these early New England communities. In any case, the contemptuous attitude of Massachusetts and her disregard of the royal commands were not forgotten; and when, a few years later, the authorities in England took up in earnest the enforcement of the new colonial policy as defined by acts of Parliament and royal orders and proclamations, the colony of Massachusetts Bay was the first to feel the weight of the royal displeasure.

CHAPTER VIII

WARS WITH THE INDIANS

THE period from 1660 to 1675, a time of readjustment in the affairs of the New England colonies, was characterized by widespread excitement and deep concern on the part of the colonies everywhere. Scarcely a section of the territory from Maine to the frontier of New York and the towns of Long Island but felt the strain of impending change in its political status. The winning of the charters and the capture of New Amsterdam were momentous events in the lives of the colonists of Rhode Island and Connecticut; while the agitation for the annexation of New Haven and the acrimonious debate that accompanied it must have stirred profoundly the towns of that colony and have led to local controversies, rivalries, and contentions that kept the inhabitants in a continual state of perturbation. On Long Island before 1664, the uncertainty as to jurisdiction, due to grave doubts as to the meaning of Connecticut's charter, aroused the towns from Easthampton and Southold on the east to Flushing and Gravesend on the west, and divided the people into discordant and clashing groups. Captain John Scott, already mentioned, an adventurer and soldier of fortune who at one time or another seems to have made trouble in nearly every part of the British world, appeared at this time in Long Island and, denying Connecticut's title to the territory, proclaimed the King. In January, 1664, he established a government at Setauket, with himself as president. This event set the towns in an uproar; Captain Young from Southold, upholding Connecticut's claim, came "with a trumpet" to Hempstead; New Haven men crossed Long Island Sound to support Scott's cause; and at last Connecticut herself sent over officers to seize the insurgents. Though Scott said he would "sacrifice his heart's blood upon the ground" before he would yield, he was taken and carried in chains to Hartford.

Both Plymouth and Massachusetts sent letters protesting against the treatment of Scott, and the heat engendered among the members of the New England Confederation was intensified by the controversy over New Haven and the "uncomfortable debates" regarding the title to the Narragansett territory. Massachusetts wrote to Connecticut in 1662, "We cannot a little wonder at your proceeding so suddenly to extend your authority to the trouble of your friends and confederates"; to which Connecticut replied, hoping that Massachusetts would stop laying further temptations before "our subjects at Mistack of disobedience to this government." The matter was debated for many years, and it was not until 1672 that Massachusetts recognized Connecticut's title under the charter and yielded, not because it thought the claim just but because "it was judged by us more dangerous to the common cause of New England to oppose than by our forbearance and yielding to endeavour to prevent a mischief to us both."

In Rhode Island conditions were equally unsettled, for the inhabitants of the border towns did not know certainly in what colony they were situated or what authority to recognize; and though these doubts affected but little the daily life of the farmer, they did affect the title to his lands and the payment of his taxes, and threw suspicion upon all legal processes and transactions. The situation was even more disturbed in the regions north of Massachusetts, where the status of Maine and New Hampshire was undecided and where the coming of the royal commissioners only served to throw the inhabitants into a new ferment. The claims of Mason and Gorges were revived by their descendants, and the King peremptorily ordered Massachusetts to surrender the provinces. Agents of Gorges appeared in the territory and demanded an acknowledgment of their authority; the commissioners themselves attempted to organize a government and to exercise jurisdiction there in the King's name; but in 1668 Massachusetts, denying all other pretensions, adopted a resolution asserting her full right of control, and, sending commissioners with a military escort to York, resumed jurisdiction of the province. The inhabitants did not know what to do. Some upheld the Gorges agents and the commissioners; others adhered to Massachusetts. Even in Massachusetts itself there were grave differences of opinion, for the younger generation did not always follow the old magistrates, and the people of Boston were developing views both of government and of the proper relations toward England that were at variance with those of the more conservative country towns and districts.

The larger disputes between the colonies were frequently accompanied with lesser disputes between the towns over their boundaries; and both at this time and for years afterwards there was scarcely an important settlement in New England that did not have some trouble with its neighbor. In 1666 Stamford and Greenwich came to blows over their dividing line, and in 1672 men from New London and Lyme attempted to mow the same piece of meadow and had a pitched battle with clubs and scythes. Not many years later the inhabitants of Windsor and Enfield "were so fiercely engag'd" over a disputed strip of land, reported an eye-witness, that a hundred men met to decide this controversy by force, "a resolute combat" ensuing between them "in which many blows were given to the exasperating each party, so that the lives and limbs of his Majesties subjects were endangered thereby."

Though clubs and scythes and fists are dangerous weapons enough, the only real fighting in which the colonists engaged was with the Indians and with weapons consisting of pikes and muskets. Indian attacks were an ever-present danger, for the stretches of unoccupied land between the colonies were the hunting-grounds of the Narragansetts of eastern Connecticut and western Rhode Island, the Pequots of Connecticut, the Wampanoags of Plymouth and its neighborhood, the Pennacooks of New Hampshire, and the Abenaki tribes of Maine. Plague and starvation had so far weakened the coast Indians before the arrival of the first colonists that the new settlements had been but little disturbed; but, unfortunately, as the first comers pushed into the interior, founding new plantations, felling trees, and clearing the soil, and the trappers and traders invaded the Indian hunting-grounds, carrying with them firearms and liquor, the Indian menace became serious.

To meet the Indian peril, all the colonies made provision for a supply of arms and for the drilling of the citizen body in militia companies or trainbands. But in equipment, discipline, and morale the fighting force of New England was very imperfect. The troops had no uniforms; there was a very inadequate commissariat; and alarums, whether by beacon, drum-beat, or discharge of guns, were slow and unreliable. Weapons were crude, and the method of handling them was exceedingly awkward and cumbersome. The pike was early abandoned and the matchlock soon gave way to the flintlock — both heavy and unwieldy instruments of war — and carbines and pistols were also used. Cavalry or mounted infantry, though expensive because of horse and outfit, were introduced whenever possible. In 1675, Plymouth had fourteen companies of infantry and cavalry; Massachusetts had six regiments, including the Ancient and Honorable Artillery; and Maine and New Hampshire had one each. Connecticut had four train-bands in 1662 and nine in 1668, a troop of dragoneers, and a troop of horse, but no regiments until the next century. For coast defense there were forts, very inadequately supplied with ordnance, of which that on Castle Island in Boston harbor was the most conspicuous, and, for the frontier, there were garrison-houses and stockades.

Though Massachusetts had twice put herself in readiness to repel attempts at coercion from England, and though both Connecticut and New Haven seemed on several occasions in danger from the Dutch, particularly after the recapture of New Amsterdam in 1673, New England's chief danger was always from the Indians. Both French and Dutch were believed to be instrumen-

tal in inciting Indian warfare, one along the
southwestern border, the other at various points
in the north, notably in New Hampshire and
Maine. But, except for occasional Indian forays
and for house-burnings and scalpings in the more
remote districts, there were only two serious wars
in the seventeenth century — that against the
Pequots in 1637 and the great War of King Philip
in 1675–1676.

The Pequot War, which was carried on by Connecticut with a few men from Massachusetts and
a number of Mohegan allies, ended in the complete
overthrow of the Pequot nation and the exter-
mination of nearly all its fighting force. It began in June, 1637, with the successful attack by
Captain John Mason on the Pequot fort near
Groton, and was brought to an end by the battle
of Fairfield Swamp, July 13, where the surviving
Pequots made their last stand. Sassacus, the
Pequot chieftain, was murdered by the Mohawks,
among whom he had sought refuge; and during
the year that followed wandering members of the
tribe, whenever found, were slain by their enemies,
the Mohegans and Narragansetts. An entire Indian people was wiped out of existence, an achieve-
ment difficult to justify on any ground save

that of the extreme necessity of either slaying or being slain. The relentless pursuit of the scattered and dispirited remnants of these tribes admits of little defense.

The overthrow of the Pequots opened to settlement the region from Saybrook to Mystic and led to a treaty in 1638 with the Mohegans and Narragansetts, according to which harmony was to prevail and peace was to reign. But the outcome of this impracticable treaty was a five years' struggle between the Mohegan chieftain, Uncas, actively allied with the colony of Connecticut, and Miantonomo, sachem of the Narragansetts, which involved Connecticut in a tortuous and often dishonorable policy of attempting to divide the Indians in order to rule them — a policy which led to many embarrassing negotiations and bloody conflicts and ended in the murder of Miantonomo in 1643, by the Mohegans, at the instigation of the commissioners of the United Colonies. This alliance between Uncas and the colony lasted for more than forty years. It placed upon Connecticut the burden of supporting a treacherous and grasping Indian chief; it created a great deal of confusion in land titles in the eastern part of the colony because of indiscriminate Indian grants;

it started the famous Mohegan controversy which agitated the colony and England also, and was not finally settled until 1773, one hundred and thirty years later; and it was, in part at least, a cause of King Philip's War, because of the colony's support of the Mohegans against their traditional enemies, the Narragansetts and Niantics.

The presence of the Indians in and near the colonies rendered frequent dealings with them a matter of necessity. The English settlers generally purchased their lands from the Indians, paying in such goods or implements or trinkets as satisfied savage need and desire. In so doing they acquired, as they supposed, a clear title of ownership, though there can be no doubt that what the Indian thought he sold was not the actual soil but only the right to occupy the land in common with himself. As the years wore on, the problems of reservations, trade, and the sale of firearms and liquor engaged the attention of the authorities and led to the passage of many laws. The conversion of the Indians to Christianity became the object of many pious efforts, and in Massachusetts and Plymouth resulted in communities of "Praying Indians," estimated in 1675 at about four thousand individuals. In contact with the white man the Indian tended to deteriorate. He frequented the settlements often to the annoyance of the men and the dread of the women and children; he got into debt, was incurably slothful and idle, and developed an uncontrollable desire to drink and steal. Where the Indians were not a menace, they were a nuisance, and the colonies passed many laws concerning the Indians which were designed to meet the one condition as well as the other.

But the real danger to New England came not from those Indians who occupied reservations and hung around the settlements, but from those who, with savage spirit unbroken, were slowly being driven from their hunting-grounds and nurtured an implacable hatred against the aggressive and relentless pioneers. The New Englanders numbered at this time some 80,000 individuals, with an adult and fighting population of perhaps 16,000; while the number of the Indians altogether may have reached as high as 12,000, with the Narragansetts, the strongest of all, mustering 4,000. The final struggle for possession of the main part of central and southern New England territory came in 1675, in what is known as King Philip's War.

Scarcely had the fears aroused by the arrival of a Dutch fleet at New York and the capture of that city been allayed by the peace of Westminster in 1674, when rumors of Indian unrest began to spread through the settlements, and the dread of Indian outbreaks began to arouse new apprehensions in the hearts of the people. Hitherto no Indian chieftain had proved himself a born leader of his people. Neither Sessaquem, Sassacus, Pumham, Uncas, nor Miantonomo had been able to quiet tribal jealousies and draw to his standard against the English others than his own immediate followers. But now appeared a sachem who was the equal of any in hatred of the white man and the superior of all in generalship, who was gifted both with the power of appeal to the younger Indians and with the finesse required to rouse other chieftains to a war of vengeance. Philip, or Metacom, was the second son of old Massasoit, the longtime friend of the English, and, upon the death of his elder brother Alexander in 1662, became the head of the Wampanoags, with his seat at Mount Hope, a promontory extending into Narragansett Bay. Believing that his people had been wronged by the English, particularly by those of Plymouth colony, and foreseeing that

he and his people were to be driven step by step
westward into narrower and more restricted quarters, he began to plot a great campaign of exter-
mination. On June 24, 1675, a body of Indians
fell on the town of Swansea, on the eastern side
of Narragansett Bay, slew nine of the inhabitants
and wounded seven others. Though assistance
was sent from Massachusetts and Plymouth, the
burning and massacring continued, extending to
Rehoboth, Taunton, and towns northward. The
settlements were isolated before the troops could
reach them, their inhabitants were slain, cabins
were burned, and prisoners were carried into captivity. The Rhode Islanders fled to the islands;
elsewhere settlers gathered in garrisoned forts and
blockhouses and in new forts hastily erected.

Though the authorities of Connecticut and
Massachusetts sent agents among the Nipmucks
hoping to prevent their alliance with Philip, the
effort failed, and by August the tribes on the upper
Connecticut had joined the movement and now began a determined and systematic destruction of the
settlements in central New England. The famous
massacre and burning of Deerfield took place on
September 12, the surviving inhabitants fleeing
to Hatfield, leaving their town in ruins. Hatfield,

Northfield, Springfield, and Westfield were attacked in turn, and though the defense was sometimes successful, more often the defenders were ambushed and killed. So widespread was the uprising that during the autumn, a desultory warfare was carried on as far north as Falmouth, Brunswick, and Casco Bay, where at least fifty Englishmen were slain by members of the Saco and Androscoggin tribes.

As yet the Narragansetts, bravest of all the southern New England Indians, whose chief was Canonchet, son of the murdered Miantonomo, had taken no part in the war. But as rumor spread that they had welcomed Philip and listened to his appeals and were probably planning to join in the murderous fray, war was declared against them on November 2, 1675, and a force of a thousand men and horse from Plymouth and Massachusetts was drawn up on Dedham plain, under the command of General Josiah Winslow and Captain Benjamin Church. On December 19, the greater part of this force, aided by troops from Connecticut, fell on the Narragansetts in their swamp fort, south of the present town of Kingston, and after a fierce and bloody fight completely routed them, though at a heavy loss. The tribe was driven from its own territory, and Canonchet fled to the Connecticut River, where he established a rallying point for new forays. His followers allied themselves with the Wampanoags and Nipmucks and began a new series of massacres. In February and March, 1676, they fell upon Lancaster, where they carried off Mrs. Rowlandson, who has left us a narrative of her captivity; upon Medfield, where fifty houses were burned; and upon Weymouth and Marlborough, which were raided and in part destroyed. Repeated assaults in other quarters kept the western frontier of Massachusetts in a frightful condition of terror; settlers were ambushed and scalped, others were tortured, and many were carried into captivity. Even the Pennacooks of southern New Hampshire were roused to action, though their share in the war was small. Here a hundred warriors sacked a village; there Indians skulking along trails and on the outskirts of towns cut off individuals and groups of individuals, shooting, scalping, and burning them. No one was safe. Again the commissioners of the United Colonies met in council and ordered a more vigorous prosecution of the campaign. More troops were levied and garrison posts fortified, but the first results were disastrous.

Captain Pierce of Scituate was ambushed at Blackstone's River near Rehoboth, and his command was completely wiped out. Sudbury was destroyed in April, and a relieving force escaped only with heavy loss.

But the strength of the Indians was waning. Canonchet, run to earth near the Pawtuxet River, was captured and sentenced to death, and his execution was entrusted to Oneko, the son of Uncas. His head was cut off and carried to Hartford, and his body was committed to the flames. The loss of Canonchet was a bitter blow to Philip, who now saw his allies falling away and himself deserted by all but a few faithful followers. The campaign — at last well in hand and directed by that prince of Indian fighters, Benjamin Church, now commissioned a colonel by General Winslow — was approaching an end. Using friendly savages as scouts, Colonel Church gradually located and captured stray bodies of Indians and brought them as captives to Plymouth. Finally, coming on the trail of Philip himself, he first intercepted his followers, and then, relentlessly pursuing the fleeing chieftain from one point to another, tracked him to his lair at his old stronghold, Mount Hope. There the great chief who had terrorized New

England for nearly a year was slain by one of
his own race. His ornaments and treasure were
seized by the soldiers, and his crown, gorget, and
two belts, all of gold and silver of Indian make,
were sent as a present to Charles II. With the
death of Philip, August 12, 1676, the whole movement collapsed, and the remaining hostile Indians,
dispersed and in flight, with their leaders gone and
starvation threatening, sought refuge among the
northern tribes. Thus the last effort to check the
English advance in southern and central New
England was brought to an end. From this time
on, the Indians in Massachusetts, Rhode Island,
and Connecticut lingered for a century and a half,
a steadily dwindling remnant, wards of the governments and occupants of reservations, until they
ceased to exist as a separate people.

The havoc wrought by the war was a great blow
to the prosperity of New England. Probably
more than six hundred whites had been slain or
captured, and hundreds of houses and a score of
villages had been burnt or pillaged; crops had
been destroyed, cattle driven off, and agriculture
in many quarters brought to a complete standstill.
In 1676, there was little leisure to sow and less
to reap. Provisions became increasingly scarce;

none could be had near at hand, for none of the colonies had a surplus; and attempts to obtain them from a distance proved unavailing. Staples for trade with the West Indies decreased; the fur trade was curtailed; and fishing was hampered for want of men. To add to the confusion, a plague vexed the colonies. It seemed to all as if the hand of God lay heavily upon New England, and days of humiliation and prayer were appointed to assuage the wrath of the Almighty. A Massachusetts act of November, 1675, ascribed the war to the judgment of God upon the colony for its sins, among which were included an excess of apparel, the wearing of long hair, and the rudeness of worship, all marks of an apostasy from the Lord "with a great backsliding." The Puritan fear of divine displeasure adds a relieving note to the general despondency and must have stiffened the determination of the orthodox leaders to resist to the utmost all attempts to liberalize the life of the colony or to alter its character as a religious state patterned after the divine plan. King Philip's War probably strengthened the position of the conservative element in Massachusetts.

CHAPTER IX

THE BAY COLONY DISCIPLINED

EXCEPT for the northern frontier, where Indian forays and atrocities continued for many years longer, the last great struggle with the Indians in New England was finished. The next danger came from a different quarter and in a different form. In June, 1676, two months before the Indian War was over, one Edward Randolph arrived from England to make an inquiry into the affairs of Massachusetts. That colony had scarcely weathered the ever-threatening peril of the New World when it was called upon to face an attack from the Old which endangered the continuance of those precious privileges for which the magistrates at Boston had contended with a vigor shrewd rather than wise. As we have seen, the position that Massachusetts assumed as a colony largely independent of British control was incompatible with England's colonial and commercial policy, a position that was certain to be called in question as soon as the authorities at home were able to give serious attention to it.

This opportunity did not arrive until, in 1674, the plantations council was dismissed, and colonial business was handed over to the Privy Council and placed in the hands of a standing committee of that body known as the Lords of Trade. This committee, which was more dignified and authoritative than had been the old council, at once assumed a firmer tone toward the colonies. It caused a proclamation to be issued announcing the royal determination to enforce the acts of trade, and it made the King's will known in America by means of new instructions to the royal governors there. It stated clearly the purpose of the Government to bring the colonies into a position of greater dependence on the Crown in the interest of the trade and revenues of the kingdom, and it showed no inclination to grant Massachusetts, with all the charges and complaints against her, preferential treatment. At the same time it was not disposed to pay much attention to religious differences, minor misdemeanors, and neighborhood quarrels, if only the colony would conform to British policy in all that concerned the

royal prerogative and the authority of Parliament;
but it made it perfectly plain that continued
infractions of parliamentary acts and royal commands would not be condoned.

Had the leaders of Massachusetts been more
complaisant and less given to a policy of evasion
and delay, it is not unlikely that the colony would
have been allowed to retain its privileges; and
had they been less absorbed in themselves and
more observant of the world outside, they might
have seen the changes that were coming over the
temper and purpose of those in England who
were shaping the relations between England and
her colonies. But Massachusetts had grown provincial since the Restoration, looking backward
rather than forward and moving in very narrow
channels of thought and life, so that she was
wrapped up in matters of purely local interest.
The clergy were struggling to maintain their
control in colony and college, while the deputies
in the legislature, representing in the main the
conservative country districts, were upholding
the clerical party against some of the magistrates,
who represented the town of Boston and were inclined to take a more liberal and progressive view
of the matter. These country members saw in

England's attitude only the desire of a despotic Stuart régime to suppress the liberties of a Puritan commonwealth, and failed to see that the investigation into the affairs of Massachusetts was but an effort to establish a colonial policy fundamental to England's welfare and power.

It cannot be said that, from 1660 to 1684, the Government in England displayed undue animus toward the colony. It allowed Massachusetts to do a great many things that in law she had no right to do, such as coining money and issuing a charter to Harvard College. Its demand for a broadening of the Massachusetts franchise was in the interest of liberty and not against it, and the insistence on freedom of worship deserves no reproof. Its condemnation of many of the Massachusetts laws as oppressive and unjust shows that in some respects legal opinion in England at this time was more advanced than that in Massachusetts and Connecticut, and, even at its worst, English law did not go to the Mosaic code for its precedents. There is a distinct note of cruelty and oppression in some of the Massachusetts and Connecticut legislation at this time, and many of the Puritan measures were harsh and arbitrary and liable to abuse. Even the Government's support of the Mason and Gorges claims was not dishonorable, and while it may have been unwise and, in equity, unjust, it was not without excuse. The Government listened to complaints of persecution, as any sovereign power is required to do, and was naturally impressed with the weightiness of some of the charges; yet so little inclined was it to tamper with Massachusetts that the colony might have succeeded, for a longer time at least, in maintaining the integrity of its control, had not the question of colonial trade brought matters to a crisis.

Under Charles II, finances presented a difficult problem, for Parliament in controlling appropriations took no responsibility for the collection of money granted. To meet the deficit which during the earlier years of the reign was ever present, efforts were made to increase the revenue from customs, and so successful was this policy that, after 1675, these customs revenues came to be looked upon as among England's greatest sources of wealth. Now, inasmuch as trade with the colonies was one of the largest factors contributing to this result, England, as she could not afford to maintain colonies that would do nothing to aid her, came more and more to value her overseas possessions for their commercial importance, classing as valuable assets those that advanced her prosperity, and treating as insubordinate those that disregarded the acts of trade and thwarted her policy. The independence that Massachusetts claimed was diametrically opposed to the growing English notion that a colony should be subordinate and dependent, should obey the acts of trade and navigation, and should recognize the authority of the Crown; and, from what they heard of the temper of New England, English statesmen suspected that Massachusetts was doing none of these things.

Edward Randolph, who was sent over in 1676 to make inquiry into the affairs of the colony, was a native of Canterbury, a former student of Gray's Inn, and at this time forty-three years old. The fact that he was connected by marriage with the Mason family accounts for his interest in the efforts of Gorges and Mason to break the hold of Massachusetts upon New Hampshire and Maine. He was a personal acquaintance of Sir Robert Southwell, the diplomatist, and of Southwell's intimate friend, William Blathwayt, an influential English official interested in the colonies. He had been in the employ of the government, and

now, probably at the instance of Southwell and
Blathwayt, he was selected to fill the difficult
and thankless post of commissioner to New England. That he had ability and courage no one
can doubt, and that he pursued his course with a
tenacity that would have won commendation in
other and less controversial fields, his career shows.
His devotion to the interests of the Crown and
his loyalty to the Church of England steeled
him against the almost incessant attacks and
rebuffs that he was called upon to endure, and
his entire inability to see any other cause than
his own saved him from the discouragements
that must certainly have broken a man more sensi-
tive than himself. He exhibited at times some
of the obduracy of the zealot and martyr; at
others he displayed unexpected good sense in
protesting against extremes of action that he
thought unjust or unwise. He was honest and
indefatigable in the pursuit of what he believed
to be his duty, and was ill-requited for his labors,
but he was a persistent fault-finder and his letters
are masterpieces of complaint. He was thrice
married, his second wife dying at the height of
his troubles in Massachusetts, and he had five
children, all daughters, one of whom proved a

grievous disappointment to him. Though he held many offices, he was always in debt and died poor, at the age of seventy, in Accomac County in Virginia. He was far from being the best man to send to New England, but his natural obstinacy and his determination to overcome difficulties were intensified by the discourteous and tactless manner in which he was received by the Puritans. He had no sympathy with the efforts of the "old faction" to save the colony, and the people of Massachusetts responded with a bitter and lasting hate.

Randolph landed at Boston on June 10, and remained in the colony until the end of July, about six weeks altogether. He visited Plymouth, New Hampshire, and Maine, interviewed men in authority and all sorts of other people, and he came to the conclusion that the majority of the inhabitants were discontented with the Boston régime. The magistrates ignored his presence as much as they dared, refusing to recognize him as anything but an enemy representing the Mason and Gorges claims, and insisting that though the King might enlarge their privileges he could not abridge them. Randolph, thoroughly nettled, returned to England prepared to do his worst.

He sent several reports to the King and constantly appeared before the Privy Council and the Lords of Trade, each time doing all the damage that he could. He had undoubtedly got much of his information from prejudiced sources or from hearsay, and he was as eager to retail it as had been the Massachusetts authorities to blast the moral character of the King's commissioners. He denounced the "old faction" as cunning, deceptive, overbearing, and disloyal; he called the clergy proud, ignorant, imperious, and inclined to sedition; and he denounced those in authority as "inconsiderable mechanicks, packed by the prevailing party of the factious ministry, with a fellow-feeling both in the command and the profits." His picture of the colony, containing much that was near the truth, was at the same time distorted, out of proportion, and in parts almost a caricature. His most effective reports were those which laid stress upon the failure of the colony to obey the navigation acts and the royal commands, and upon its use of the word "Commonwealth," as if the corporation were already an independent state. These reports were accepted by the English authorities as correct statements of fact, for they seemed to be confirmed by the evidence of London merchants and by at least one West Indian governor, who knew the colony and had no personal interests at stake.

In October, 1676, Massachusetts sent over two of its leading men, William Stoughton, a magistrate, and Peter Bulkeley, speaker of the House of Representatives, to ward off, if possible, the attack on the colony, but with characteristic short-sightedness gave them no authority to discuss officially anything but the Mason and Gorges claims. For more than two years these men, representative rather of the moderate party than of the "old faction" in the colony, remained in England, frequently appearing before the Lords of Trade, where they were subjected to a searching examination at the hands of a not very sympathetic body of men. The meetings in the Council Chamber in Whitehall, where the committee sat, were occasions full of interest and excitement. At one of them, on April 8, 1677, Stoughton, Bulkeley, Randolph, Mason, and Sir Edmund Andros, Governor of New York for the Duke, were all present, and the agents must have found the situation awkward and embarrassing. The committee expressed its resentment at the colony's habit of disobedience and evasion, and showed

no inclination to adopt a moderate policy, advo-
cating, on the contrary, investigation "from the
whole root." The position of a Massachusetts
agent in England during these trying years was
most undesirable, and so many difficulties and
discouragements did Stoughton and Bulkeley
encounter that several times they asked for permission to return home and once, at least, had
to go to the country for their health. But whatever were the troubles of an agent in England,
they were trifling as compared with those which
confronted him at home when he failed, as he
almost invariably did fail, to obtain all that the
colony expected. Cotton Mather tells us that
Norton died in 1663 of melancholy and chagrin,
and that for forty years there was not one agent
but met "with some very froward entertainment
among his countrymen." No wonder it was always difficult to find men who were willing to go.

At first the Lords of Trade favored the sending
of a supplemental charter and the extending of a
pardon to the colony; but as the evidence against
Massachusetts accumulated, they began to consider the revision of the laws, the appointment of
a collector of customs and a royal governor, and
even the annulment of the charter itself. In

short, they determined to bring Massachusetts "under a more palpable declaration of obedience to his Majesty." The general court of the colony, although it had said that "any breach in the wall would endanger the whole," was at last frightened by the news from England and passed an order in October, 1677, that the laws of trade must be strictly observed, and later magistrates and deputies alike took the oath of allegiance prescribed by the Crown, promising to drop the word "Commonwealth" for the future. The members of the assembly wrote an amazing letter, pietistic and cringing, in which they prostrated themselves before the King, asked to be numbered among his "poore yet humble and loyal subjects," and begged for a renewal of all their privileges. At best such a letter could have done little in England to increase respect for the colony, but any good results expected from it were completely destroyed by the serious blunder which the colony made at this time in purchasing from the Gorges claimants the title to the province of Maine, which with New Hampshire had recently been declared by the chief justices of the King's Bench and Common Pleas to lie outside of the jurisdiction of Massachusetts. This attempt to obtain, without the royal

consent, a territory which the legal advisers of
the Crown had decided Massachusetts could not
have, only strengthened the determination of the
authorities in England to bring the colony into
the King's hand by the appointment of a royal
governor. For the moment, however, the uprising of Bacon in Virginia and the Popish Plot in
England so distracted the Government that it
was obliged to slight or to postpone much of its
business. It did succeed in settling the perplex-
ing question of New Hampshire, for, having obtained from Mason a renunciation of all his claims
to the Government, though leaving him with full
title to the soil, it organized that territory as a
colony under the control of the Crown.

With these matters out of the way or less exi-
gent, the Lords of Trade returned to the affairs of
New England. They wished, before proceeding to
extremes, to give Massachusetts another chance to
be heard; so, in dismissing the agents in the autumn
of 1679, they instructed the colony to send over
within six months others fully prepared "to answer
the misdemeanors imputed against them." They
also decided to send Randolph back as collector
and surveyor of customs, with letters to all the
New England colonies, ordering them to enforce

the acts of trade, and another to Massachusetts requiring that she provide a minister for those in Boston who wished an Anglican church. Randolph, who left for New England for the second time, in December, 1678, has the distinction of being the first royal official appointed for any of the northern colonies. Almost his first task was to settle the province of New Hampshire under royal authority, with a government consisting of a president, a council, and an assembly. Thus British control in New England was making progress, and the worst fears of the "old faction" in Massachusetts were being realized.

It is difficult to understand the attitude of Massachusetts. Her leaders probably thought that with the settlement of the Mason and Gorges claims the most serious source of trouble with England was disposed of. They believed, honestly enough, though the wish was father to the thought, that the colony lay beyond the reach of Parliament and that the laws of England were bounded by the four seas and did not reach America. Hence they deemed the navigation acts an invasion of their liberties and could not bring themselves to obey them. As to England's new colonial policy, it is doubtful if they grasped it at all,

or would have acknowledged it as applicable to themselves, even if they had understood it. The experiences and reports of their agents in England seem to have taught them nothing and served only to confirm their belief that a Stuart was a tyrant and that all English authorities were natural enemies. They had labored and suffered in the vineyard of the Lord and they wished to be let alone to enjoy their dearly won privileges. Randolph wrote, soon after his arrival in New England, that the colony was acting "as high as ever," and that "it was in every one's mouth that they are not subject to the laws of England nor were such laws in force until confirmed by their authority." The colony neglected to send the agents demanded, alleging expense, the dangers of the sea, the difficulty of finding any one to accept the post, and their belief that King and council were "taken up with matters of greater importance," until finally in September, 1680, the King wrote an exceedingly sharp letter, calling the excuses "insufficient pretences," and commanding that agents be sent within three months. Strange to say the colony even then allowed a year to elapse before complying, and again instructed those whom they sent to agree to nothing that concerned the charter.

Before the agents arrived in the summer of 1682, the royal patience was exhausted. Randolph's continued complaints that he was obstructed in every way in the performance of his duties; the act of the colony in setting up a naval office of its own; the revival of an old law imposing the death penalty upon any one who should "attempt the alteration or subversion of the frame of government"; the opinion of the Attorney-General that the colony had done quite enough to warrant the forfeiture of its charter; and the delay in sending the agents, which seemed a further flouting of the royal commands — all these things brought matters to a crisis. Therefore, when finally the Massachusetts agents reached England, they found the situation hopeless. "It is a hard service we are engaged in," they wrote; "we stand in need of help from Heaven." Their want of powers provoked the Lords of Trade to say that unless they were procured, the charter would be forfeited at once. Randolph was called back in May, 1683, to aid in the legal proceedings which were immediately set on foot. Other charters were falling: that of the Bermuda Company was under attack; that of the City of London was already forfeited; and those of other

English boroughs were in danger.   On June 27,
a writ of *quo warranto* was issued out of the Court
of King's Bench against the colony.   The agents,
refusing to defend the suit, returned to New England, and the writ was given to Randolph to serve.
He reached Boston in October, but owing to de-
lays in the colony and a tempestuous voyage
back, he was unable to return it to England
within the allotted time.   The first attempt failed,
but another was soon made.   By the advice of the
Attorney-General, suit was brought in the Court
of Chancery by writ of *scire facias* against the
company, and upon the rendering of judgment
for non-appearance the charter was declared forfeited on October 23, 1684.

Though the colony was given no opportunity
to defend the suit, the charter was legally vacated
according to the forms of English law. The colony
was but a corporation, its charter but a corporation
charter, and in only one respect did it differ from
other corporations, namely, its residence in America. The methods of vacating corporate charters
in England were definite and in this case were
strictly followed.   Had Massachusetts been a corporation in fact as well as in law, it is doubtful
if the question of illegality would ever have been

raised; but as this particular corporation was a Puritan commonwealth, the issue was so vital to its continuance as to lead to the charge of unjust and illegal oppression. On moral grounds a defence of the colony is always possible, though it is difficult to uphold the Massachusetts system. It was certainly neither popular nor democratic, tolerant nor progressive, and in any case it must eventually have undergone transformation from within. The city of Boston was increasing in wealth and importance, and trade was bringing it into ever closer contact with the outside world. There were growing up in the colony more open-minded and progressive men who were opposing the dominance of the country party, which found its last governor in Leverett, its chief advocates among the clergy, and its strength in the House of Representatives, and which wished to preserve things as they always had been. The leaders of this conservative party, Danforth, Nowell, Cooke, and others, struggled courageously against all concessions, but they were bound to be beaten in the end.

That the conservative members of the colony were thoroughly in earnest and thoroughly convinced of the absolute righteousness of their position, admits of no doubt. No man could speak of the loss of the charter as a breach in the "Hedge which kept us from the Wild Beasts of the Field," as did Cotton Mather, without expressing a fear of a Stuart, of an Anglican, and of a Papist that was as real as the terrors of witchcraft. To the orthodox Puritans, the preservation of their religious doctrines and government and the maintenance of their moral and social standards were a duty to God, and to admit change was a sin against the divine command. But such an unyielding system could not last; in fact, it was already giving way. Though conjecture is difficult, it seems likely that the English interference delayed rather than hastened the natural growth and transformation of the colony, because it united moderates and irreconcilables against a common enemy — the authority of the Crown.

CHAPTER X

THE ANDROS RÉGIME IN NEW ENGLAND

WITHOUT a charter Massachusetts stood bereft of her privileges and at the mercy of the royal will. She was now a royal colony, immediately under the control of the Crown and likely to receive a royal governor and a royal administration, as had other royal colonies. But the actual form that reconstruction took in New England was peculiar and rendered the conditions there unlike those in any other royal colony in America. The territory was enlarged by including New Hampshire, which was already in the King's hands, Plymouth, which was at the King's mercy because it had no charter, Maine, and the Narragansett country. Eventually there were added Connecticut, Rhode Island, New York, and the Jerseys — eight colonies in all, a veritable British dominion beyond the seas. For its Governor, Colonel Percy Kirke, recently returned from Tangier, was considered,

but Randolph, whose advice was asked, knowing
that a man like Kirke, "short-tempered, rough-
spoken, and dissolute," would not succeed, urged
that his name be withdrawn. It was agreed that
the Governor should have a council, and at first
the Lords of Trade recommended a popular
assembly, whenever the Governor saw fit; but in
this important particular they were overborne by
the Crown. After debate in a cabinet council, it
was determined "not to subject the Governor
and council to convoke general assemblies of the
people, for the purpose of laying on taxes and
regulating other matters of importance." This
unfortunate decision was a characteristic Stuart
blunder for which the Duke of York (afterwards
James II), Lord Jeffreys (not yet Lord Chancellor),
and other ministers were responsible. Kirke,
Jeffreys, and the Duke of York may well have
seemed to Cotton Mather "Wild Beasts of the
Field," dangerous to be entrusted with the shaping
of the affairs of a Puritan commonwealth.

The death of Charles II in February, 1685,
postponed action in England, and in Massachusetts the government went on as usual, the elections taking place and deputies meeting, though
with manifest half-heartedness. Randolph was

able to prevent the sending of Kirke, and finally succeeded in persuading the authorities that it would be a good plan to set up a temporary government, while they were making up their minds whom to appoint as a permanent governor-general of the new dominion. He obtained a commission as President for Joseph Dudley, son of the former Governor, an ambitious man, with little sympathy for the old faction and friendly to the idea of broadening the life of the colony by fostering closer relations with England. Randolph himself received an appointment as register and secretary of the colony, and for once in his life seemed riding to fortune on the high tide of prosperity. In 1685, he obtained nearly £500 for his services and for his losses up to that date; and when the following January he started on his fifth voyage to New England, he bore with him not only the judgment against the charter, the commission to Dudley as President, and two writs of *quo warranto* against Connecticut and Rhode Island, but also a sheaf of offices for himself — secretary, postmaster, collector of customs. He was later to become deputy-auditor and surveyor of the woods. With him went also the Reverend Robert Ratcliffe, rector of the first Anglican church

set up in Boston.   Just a week after the arrival of
Randolph and Ratcliffe in Boston, the old assembly met for the last time, and on May 21, 1686,
voted its adjournment with the pious hope, destined to be unfulfilled, that it would meet again
the following October.   The Massachusetts leaders seem almost to have believed in a miraculous
intervention of Providence to thwart the purposes of their enemy.

The preliminary government lasted but six
months and altered the life of the people but little.
For "Governor and Company" was substituted
"President and Council," a more modish name,
as some one said, but not necessarily one that
savored of despotism.   But however conciliatory
Dudley might wish to be, his acceptance of a royal
commission rankled in the minds of his countrymen; and his ability, his friendly policy, his desire
to leave things pretty much as they had been,
counted for nothing because of his compact with
the enemy.   In the opinion of the old guard, he
had forsaken his birthright and had turned traitor
to the land of his origin.   Time has modified this
judgment and has shown that, however unlovely
Dudley was in personal character and however
lacking he was at all times in self-control, he was

an able administrator, of a type common enough
in other colonies, particularly in the next century,
serving both colony and mother country alike
and linking the two in a common bond. Under
him and his council Massachusetts suffered no
hardships. He confirmed all existing arrange-
ments regarding land, taxes, and town organization, and, knowing Massachusetts and the temper
of her people as well as he did, he took pains to
write to the King that it would be helpful to all
concerned if the Government could have a representative assembly. To grant the people a share
in government would, he believed, appease discontent on one side and help to fill an empty
treasury on the other; but nothing came of his
suggestion.

Throughout New England as a whole, the daily
routine of life was pursued without regard to
the particular form of government established in
Boston. In Massachusetts the election of deputies stopped, but in other respects the town meetings carried on their usual business. In other
colonies no changes whatever took place. Men
tilled the soil, went to church, gathered in town
meetings, and ordered their ordinary affairs as they
had done for half a century. The seaports felt

the change more than did the inland towns, for the enforcement of the navigation acts interfered somewhat with the old channels of trade and led to the introduction of a court of vice-admiralty which Dudley held for the first time in July to try ships engaged in illicit trade. Over the forts and the royal offices fluttered a new flag, bearing a St. George's cross on a white field, with the initials J. R. and a crown embroidered in gold in the center of the cross, that same cross which Endecott had cut from the flag half a century before. To many the new flag was the symbol of anti-Christ, and Cotton Mather judged it a sin to have the cross restored; but others felt with Sewall, the diarist, who said of the fall of the old government: "The foundations being destroyed, what can the righteous do?"

Perhaps the greatest innovation — in any case, the novelty that aroused the largest amount of curiosity and excitement — was the service according to the Book of Common Prayer, held at first in the library room of the Town House, and afterwards by arrangement in the South Church, and conducted by the Reverend Robert Ratcliffe in a surplice, before a congregation composed not only of professed Anglicans but also of many men of

Boston who had never before seen the Church of England form of worship. The Anglican rector, by his somewhat unfortunate habit of running over the time allowance and keeping the waiting Congregationalists from entering their own church for the enjoyment of their own form of worship, caused almost as much discontent as did the dancing-master of whom the ministers had complained the year before, who set his appointments on Lecture days and declared that by one play he could teach more divinity than Mr. Willard or the Old Testament. Other "provoking evils" show that not all the breaches in the walls were due to outside attacks. A list of twelve such evils was drawn up in 1675, and the crimes which were condemned, and which were said to be committed chiefly by the younger sort, included immodest wearing of the hair by men, strange new fashions of dress, want of reverence at worship, profane cursing, tippling, breaking the Sabbath, idleness, overcharges by the merchants, and the "loose and sinful habit of riding from town to town, men and women together, under pretence of going to lectures, but really to drink and revel in taverns." The law forbidding the keeping of Christmas Day had to be repealed in 1681.

Mrs. Randolph, when attending Mr. Willard's preaching at the South Church, was observed "to make a curtsey" at the name of Jesus "even in prayer time"; and the colony was threatened with "gynecandrical or that which is commonly called Mixt or Promiscuous Dancing," and with marriage according to the form of the Established Church. The old order was changing, but not without producing friction and bitterness of spirit. The orthodox brethren stigmatized Ratcliffe as "Baal's priest," and the ministers from their pulpits denounced the Anglican prayers as "leeks, garlick, and trash." The upholders of the covenant were convinced that already "the Wild Beasts of the Field" were assailing the colony.

Randolph journeyed on horseback twice to Rhode Island, and once to Connecticut, serving his writs upon those colonies. Rhode Island agreed willingly enough to surrender her charter without a suit, but the authorities of Connecticut, knowing that the time for the return of the writ had expired, gave no answer, debating among themselves whether it would not be better, if they had to give in, to join New York rather than Massachusetts. Randolph attributed their hesitation to their dislike of Dudley, for whom he had begun to entertain an intense aversion. He charged Dudley with connivance against himself, interference with his work, appropriation of his fees, and too great friendliness toward the old faction in Boston. Before the provisional government had come to an end, he was writing home that Dudley was a "false president," conducting affairs in his private interest, a lukewarm supporter of the Anglican church, a backslider from his Majesty's service, turning "windmill-like to every gale." Such was Dudley's fate in an era of transition — hated by the old faction as an appointee of the Stuarts and by Randolph as a weak servant of the Crown. Writing in November, Randolph longed for the coming of the real governor, who would put a check upon the country party and bring to an end the time-serving and trimming of a president whom he deemed no better than a Puritan governor.

The new Governor-General, who entered Boston harbor in the *Kingfisher* on December 19, 1686, was Sir Edmund Andros, a few years before the Duke of York's Governor for the propriety of New York. Andros at this time was forty-nine years old; he was a soldier by training and a man of considerable experience in positions requiring executive ability.   His career had been an honorable one, and no charges involving his honesty, loyalty, or personal conduct had ever been entered against him.   When he was in New York, he had been brought on several occasions into contact with the Massachusetts leaders, and though their relations had never been sympathetic, they had not been unfriendly.   While in England from 1681 to 1686, he had been freely consulted regarding the best method of dealing with the problems in America and had shown himself in full accord with that policy of the Lords of Trade which attempted to consolidate the northern colonies into a single government for the execution of the acts of trade and defense against the encroachments of the French and Indians.   He was probably fully aware of the difficulties that confronted the new experiment, but as a soldier he was ready to obey orders.   His natural disposition and military training rendered him impatient of obstacles, and his unfamiliarity with any form of popular government — for New York had been controlled by a governor and council only — made extremely uncertain his success in New England, where affairs had been managed by the easy-going, dilatory method of debate and discussion.   As a disciplinarian, he could not appreciate the New Englander's fondness for disputation and argument; as a soldier, he was certain to obey to the full the letter of his instructions; and, as an Anglican, he was likely to favor the church and churchmen of his choice. He was not a diplomat, nor was he gifted with the silver tongue of oratory or the spirit of compromise. He came to New England to execute a definite plan, and he was given no discretion as to the form of government he was to set up. He and his advisory council were to make the laws, levy taxes, exercise justice, and command the militia. He was not allowed to call a popular assembly or to recognize in any way the highly prized institutions of the colony.

On December 20, Andros, his officers, and guard, clad in the brilliant uniforms of soldiers of the British establishment, landed at Leverett's wharf and marched through the local militia up King's Street to the Town House, where he read his commission and administered the oaths. Except for the royal commissioners of 1664, no British officer or soldier had hitherto set foot on the streets of Boston. Redcoats had been sent to New York and Virginia, but never before had they appeared in New England, and this visible sign of British

Cottonus Matherus
S. Theologiæ Doctor Regiæ Societatis Londinensis Socius
Ecclesiæ apud Bostonum Nov Anglorum nuper Præpositus
Ætatis Suæ LXV. MDCCXXVII.

authority must have seemed to many ominous for the future.

Andros's early impressions of what he saw were not flattering to the colony. He found the people still suffering from the devastating effects of the late war and further harassed by bad harvests, disasters at sea, and two serious fires which had recently done much damage in the city. He found the fortifications in bad repair, almost all the gun-carriages unserviceable, no magazines of powder or other stores of war, no small arms, except a few old matchlocks, and those unsizable and in poor condition, no storehouses or accommodations for officers or soldiers, and no adequate ramparts or redoubts.

Now the work that Andros had come over to perform, and that which was most important in his eyes, was the defense of New England against the French. The contest between the two nations for control of the New World had already begun. The territory between Hudson Bay and the St. Lawrence and that between the Penobscot and the St. Croix were already in dispute, and New Englanders had taken their part in the conflict. When Governor of New York, Andros had become aware of the French danger, and his successor

12

Dongan had proved himself capable of holding the Iroquois Indians to their allegiance to the English and of extending the beaver trade in the Mohawk Valley. But at this juncture reports kept coming in of renewed incursions of the French, led by the Canadian nobility, into the regions south of Lakes Erie and Ontario, and of new forts on territory that the English claimed as their own. There was increasing danger that the French would embroil the Indians of the Five Nations and, by drawing them into a French alliance, threaten not only the fur trade but the colonies themselves. The French Governor, Denonville, declared that the design of the King his master was the conversion of the infidels and the uniting of "all these barbarous people in the bosom of the Church"; but Dongan, though himself a Roman Catholic, saw no truth in this explanation and demanded that the French demolish their forts and retire to Canada, whence they had come. Just as this quarrel with the French threatened to arouse the Indians in northwestern New York, so it threatened to arouse, as eventually it did arouse, the Indians along the northern frontier of New England. To the authorities in England and to Andros in America, this menace of French

aggression was one of the dangers which the
Dominion of New England was intended to meet,
and the substitution of a single civil and military
head for the slow-moving and ineffective popular
assemblies was designed to make possible an
energetic military campaign.

Andros had no sooner organized his council and
got his government into running order than he
began to prosecute measures for improving the
defenses of the colony. He sent soldiers to Pemaquid to occupy and strengthen the fort there,
and himself began the reconstruction of the fortifications of Boston. He turned his attention to
Fort Hill at the lower end of the town, erected
a palisaded embankment with four bastions, a
house for the garrison, and a place for a battery;
later he leveled the hill on Castle Island in the
harbor, and built there a similar palisade and
earthwork and barracks for the soldiers. He took
a survey of military stores, made application to
England for guns and ammunition, endeavored to
put the train-bands of the colony in as good shape
as possible, and in 1688 went to Pemaquid to
inspect the northern defenses as far as the Penobscot. He kept in close touch with Governor
Dongan, and promised to send him, as rapidly

as he could, men and money in case of a French invasion.

To make his work more effective he took steps to bring Connecticut immediately under his control. Rhode Island had already submitted and had sent its members to sit with the council at Boston. But Connecticut had avoided giving a direct answer, although a third writ of *quo warranto* had been served upon her, on December 28, 1686. Consequently Andros wrote to the recalcitrant colony, saying that he had been instructed to receive the surrender of the charter. To this letter, the Governor and magistrates of Connecticut replied that they preferred to remain as they were, but that, if annexation was to be their lot, they would be willing to join with Massachusetts, their old neighbor and friend, rather than with New York. Dongan, perplexed by the heavy expenses involved in the military defense of his colony and wishing to have the use of additional revenues, had hoped that he might persuade the Connecticut Government to come under the control of New York, but Connecticut preferred Massachusetts and had stated this preference in her letter. Andros and the Lords of Trade deemed the reply favorable, although in fact it was ingeniously noncommittal, and they took steps to complete the annexation.

On receiving a special letter of instructions from the King, Andros set out in person for Hartford, accompanied by a number of gentlemen, two trumpeters, and a guard of fifteen or twenty redcoats, "with small guns and short lances in the tops of them." He journeyed probably by way of Norwich, crossing the Connecticut River at Wethersfield, where he was met by a troop of sixty cavalry and escorted to Hartford. There, on October 31, 1687, the Governor, magistrates, and militia awaited his coming. Seated in the Governor's chair in the tavern chamber where the assembly was accustomed to meet, he caused his commission to be read, declared the old Government dissolved, selected two of those present as members of his council, and the next day appointed the necessary officials for the colony. Thence he went to Fairfield, New Haven, and New London, commissioning justices of the peace for those counties and organizing the customs service. No resistance was made to his proceedings, though it was generally understood in the colony that the charter itself had been spirited away and hidden in the hollow of an oak tree, henceforth famous as the Charter Oak.

Connecticut and the other colonies became for the time being administrative districts of the larger dominion. Their assemblies everywhere ceased to meet, that of Rhode Island for five years. Courts, provided by the act of December, 1687, were, however, generally held. The superior court for Connecticut sat four times in 1688 and the county courts, quarter sessions and common pleas, where appeared the newly appointed justices of the peace, sat for Hartford County, the one ten times and the other thirteen times during 1688 and 1689. But the surviving records of their meetings are few and references to their work very rare. The ordinary business of everyday life was carried on by the towns alone, which continued their usual activities undisturbed. In Connecticut, before Andros arrived, the assembly had taken the precaution to issue formal patents of land to the towns and to grant the public lands of the colony to Hartford and Windsor to prevent their falling into the hands of the new Government. This act may at the time have seemed a wise one, but it made a great deal of trouble afterwards.

The Dominion of New England, which now extended from the Penobscot to the borders of New York, was organized as a centralized government, with the old colonies serving as counties for administration and the exercise of justice. But as plans for an expedition against the French began to mature, it became evident that, if the French were to be successfully met, a further extension of territory was necessary; so in April, 1688, a second commission was issued to Andros, constituting him Governor of all the territory from the St. Croix River to the fortieth parallel, and thus adding to his domain New York and the Jerseys. Delaware and Pennsylvania were excepted by special royal intervention. Dongan was recalled, and Francis Nicholson was appointed lieutenant-governor under Andros, with his residence in New York.

Thus on paper Andros was Governor-General of a single territory running from the Delaware River and the northern boundary of Pennsylvania northward to the St. Lawrence, eastward to the St. Croix, and westward to the Pacific. There was an attempt here to reproduce, in size and organization, the French Dominion of Canada, but the likeness was only in appearance. To organize and defend his territory, Andros had two companies of British regulars, half a dozen trained officers, the local train-bands, which were not to be depended on for distant service, and a meager supply of guns and ammunition. Instead of having under him a body of colonials, such as were the belligerent gentlemen of Canada, who were eager to take part in raids against the English and who led their savage followers with the craft of the redskin and the intelligence of the white man, he had many separate groups of people. Averse to war and accustomed to govern themselves, most of these distrusted him and wanted to be rid of him, and desired only the restoration of their old governments without regard to those dangers which they were fully convinced they could meet quite as well themselves.

Though Andros's authority stretched over such an enormous territory, his actual government was confined to Massachusetts and the northern frontier. He paid very little attention to Connecticut, Plymouth, and Rhode Island. With but two or three exceptions, the meetings of his council were held in Boston; the laws passed affected the people of that colony; and the complaints against him were chiefly of Massachusetts origin. Massachusetts was his real enemy, and it was Massachusetts that finally overthrew him. Andros was a soldier who never forgot the main object of his mission, and it is hardly surprising that he showed neither tact nor patience in his dealings with a colony that did little else but check and thwart the plans that had been entrusted to him for execution. The people of Massachusetts charged him with tyranny and despotism. Their leaders, many of whom were members of his council, complained of the council proceedings, which, they said, were controlled by Andros and his favorites, so that debate was curtailed, objections were overruled, and the vote of the majority was ignored. There is much truth in the charge, for Andros was self-willed, imperious, and impatient of discussion. On the other hand the Puritan leaders inordinately loved controversy and debate. If Andros was peremptory, the Puritan councillors were obstructive.

A more legitimate charge was the absence of a representative assembly and the levying of taxes by the fiat of the council. But Andros had no choice in this matter: he was compelled to govern according to his instructions. Not only was his treasury usually empty, but he was always confronted with the heavy expense of fortification and of protecting the frontier. He does not appear to have been excessive in his demands, and in case of any unusual levies, as of duties and customs, he referred the matter to the Crown for its consent. But, as Englishmen, the people preferred to levy their own taxes and considered any other method of imposition as contrary to their just rights. Andros consequently had a great deal of trouble in raising money.   Even in the council, tax laws were passed with difficulty, and the people of Essex County, notably in town meetings at Topsfield and Ipswich, protested vigorously against the levying of a rate without the consent of an assembly.   John Wise, the Ipswich minister, and others were arrested and thrown into jail, and on trial Wise, according to his own report of the matter, was told by Dudley, the chief-justice, "You have no more privileges left you than to be sold as slaves." Wise was fined and suspended from the ministry, and it is possible that his recollection of events was affected by the punishment imposed.

In the matter of property, land titles, quit-rents, and fees, the colonists had warrant for their criticism and their displeasure.   Many of those whom Andros associated with himself were New Yorkers who had served with considerable success in their former positions, but who had all the characteristics of typical royal officials.   To the average English officeholder of the seventeenth and eighteenth centuries, office was considered not merely an opportunity for service but also an opportunity for profit. Hitherto Massachusetts had been free from men of this class, common enough elsewhere and destined to become more common as the royal colonies increased in number. Palmer, the judge, Graham, the attorney-general, and West, the secretary, hardly deserve the stigma of placemen, for they possessed ability and did their duty as they saw it, but their standards of duty were different from those held in Massachusetts. People in England did not at this time view public office as a public trust, which is a modern idea. Appointments under the Crown went by purchase or favor, and, once obtained, were a source of income, a form of investment. Massachusetts and other New England colonies were far ahead of their time in giving shape to the principle that a public official was the servant of those who elected him, but to such men as Randolph and West and the whole office-holding world of this period, such an idea was unthinkable. They served the King and for their service were to receive their reward, and such men in America looked on fees and grants of land as legitimate

perquisites. In New York they had been able
to gratify their needs, but in Massachusetts such
a view of office ran counter to the traditions and
customs of the place, and attempts to apply it
caused resentment and indignation. The efforts
of these men, among whom Randolph was the
prince of beggars, to obtain grants of land, to
destroy the validity of existing titles, to levy quit-
rents, and to exact heavy fees, were a menace to
the prosperity of the colony; while the further
attempt to destroy the political importance of
the towns by prohibiting town meetings, except
once a year, was an attack on one of the most
fundamental parts of the whole New England
system. Andros himself, though laboring to break
the resisting power of the colony, never used his
office for purposes of gain.

That the Massachusetts people should oppose
these attempts to alter the methods of government which had been in vogue for half a century was inevitable, though some of the means
they employed were certainly disingenuous. Their
leaders, both lay and clerical, were unsurpassed
in genius for argument and at this time outdid
themselves. When Palmer was able to show that,
according to English law, their land-titles were

in many cases defective, they fell back on an older
title than that of the Crown and derived their
right from God, "according to his Grand Charter
to the Sons of Adam and Noah." More culpable
was the revival of the unfortunate habit of mis-
representation and calumny which had too often
characterized the treatment of the enemy in
Boston, and the spreading of rumors that Andros,
who spent a part of the winter of 1688–1689 in
Maine taking measures for defense, was in league
with the French and was furnishing the Indians
with arms and ammunition for use against the
English. Such reports represent perhaps merely
the desperate and half-hysterical methods of a
people who did not know where to turn for
the protection of their institutions. A wiser and
shrewder move was made in the spring of 1688,
when a group of prominent men determined to
appeal to England for relief and sent Increase
Mather, the influential pastor of the old North
Church, across the ocean to plead their cause with
the Crown.

But relief was nearer than they expected. On
November 5, 1688, William of Orange, summoned
from Holland to uphold the constitutional liberties of Protestant England, landed at Torbay, and

before the end of the year James II had fled to
France.   Rumors of the projected invasion had
come to Boston as early as December, and reports
of its success had reached the ears of the people
there during the March following.   Finally on
April 4, John Winslow, arriving from Nevis,
brought written copies of the Prince's declaration, issued from Holland, and two weeks later,
on April 18, the leaders in the city, including many
members of Andros's council, supported by the
people of Boston and its neighborhood, rose in
revolt, overthrew the government of Andros, and
brought tumbling down the whole structure of the
Dominion of New England, which had never from
the beginning had any real or stable foundation.
Having armed themselves, they seized Captain
George, commander of the royal frigate, the *Rose*,
lying in the harbor, as he came ashore to find out
the cause of the noise and the tumult.   Then they
moved on to Fort Hill, where Andros, Randolph,
and others had taken refuge.   Here they defied
the soldiers, who refused to fire, captured the fort,
and carried their prisoners off to be lodged in private
houses or the common jail.   On the following day,
they forced the Castle Island fort in the harbor
to surrender and then imprisoned its commander;

they demanded of the lieutenant in charge the delivery of the royal frigate and carried off the sails; and as nothing would satisfy the country people who came armed into the town in the afternoon but the closer confinement of Andros, they removed him from the private house where he had been lodged to the fort in the town. So excited was the populace and so serious the danger of injury to those in confinement, that West, Palmer, and Graham were sent to the fort on Castle Island for protection; Andros, after two futile attempts at escape, was lodged in the same quarters, while Randolph, as deserving of no consideration, was thrust ignominiously into jail. On the third day a council of safety, consisting of thirty-seven members, with the old Governor, Bradstreet, eighty-six years old, at its head, was organized to prepare the way for the reëstablishment of the former Government. The council summoned a convention which, after hesitation and delay, authorized elections for a House of Representatives and the resumption of all the old forms and powers. On June 6, the assembly met, and to all appearances Massachusetts was once more governing herself as if the charter had never been annulled.

The other colonies followed the example of Massachusetts, and miniature revolutions took place in Plymouth, Rhode Island, and Connecticut, where the Andros commissions offered few obstacles to the renewal of the old forms. In a majority of cases the old officials were at hand, ready to take up their former duties. Plymouth, having no charter, simply returned to her old way of life, precarious and uncertain as it was; but Rhode Island and Connecticut took the position that as their charters had not been vacated by law, they were still valid and had not been impaired by the brief intermission in the governments provided by them. In this opinion the colonies were upheld by the law officers in England. Before the middle of the summer, practically all traces of the Andros régime had disappeared, except for the prisoners in confinement at Boston and the bitterness which still rankled in the hearts of the people of Massachusetts. There was no such intensity of feeling in the other colonies, where the loss of the assembly was the main grievance, though in Connecticut the resumption of authority by the old leaders roused the animosity of a small but energetic faction which said that the charter was dead and could

Job Vander
Spijk. 1688.

not be revived, and demanded a closer dependence on the Crown. Henceforth, that colony had to reckon with a hostile group within its own borders, one that deemed the institutions and laws of the colony oppressive and unjust, and that for a time resisted the authority of what its leaders called a "pretended" government. During the years that followed, these men made many efforts to break down the independence of the corporate government, and to this extent the rule of Andros left a permanent mark upon the colony.

13

CHAPTER XI

THE END OF AN ERA

But the future of the New England colonies was to be decided in England and not in America. If the orthodox leaders in the colony thought that the new King had levelling sympathies or would thrust aside the policy already adopted by the English authorities for the defense of the colonies and the maintenance of the acts of trade, they greatly misjudged the situation. King William, though a Protestant, was no lover of revolution, and, though he had himself engaged in one, he could assert the dignity of the prerogative with as much vigor as any Stuart. He was not a politician, but a soldier, and he was quite as likely to see the necessity of organizing New England for defense against the enemy as he was to listen favorably to appeals from Massachusetts for a restoration of her charter.

Increase Mather had gone to England in 1688

to petition James II for relief from the burdens of
the Andros rule.   His impressive personality, his
power as a ready and forcible speaker, his resource-
fulness and energy, and his acquaintance with
influential men in England, both Anglicans and
Dissenters, made him the most effective agent
who had ever gone to England in the interest of
the colony.   He was able to bring the grievances
of Massachusetts to the personal attention of
James II; and he had received hope of a confirmation of land titles and permission to call a general
assembly, when the flight of the King brought his
efforts to naught.   He then turned to the new
Parliament, hoping to save the colony by means
of a rider to the bill for restoring corporations to
their ancient rights and privileges; but the dissolution of this body ended hopeful efforts in
that direction also.   A year's "Sisyphean labor"
came to nothing.   No remedy remained except an
appeal to the new King, and during 1690 and 1691,
the reconstruction of Massachusetts became one
of the most important questions brought before
the Lords of Trade.   William III and his advisers
were agreed on one point: that Massachusetts
should never again be independent as she formerly
had been, but should be brought within the

immediate control of the Crown, through a governor of the King's appointment. They took the ground that, with a French war already begun, it was no time to discuss colonial rights and privileges, for the demands of the empire took precedence over all questions of a merely local character in America.

Andros was now recalled and instructions were sent to Massachusetts to release all her prisoners. With their arrival in England in February, 1690, the debate before the committee went on in a new and livelier fashion. Randolph renewed his complaints in every form known to his inventive mind; Andros presented his defense and was relieved of all charges of mal-administration; Mather and others contested every move of their opponents and sought to obtain as favorable terms as possible for Massachusetts; while Oakes and Cooke, sent over by the colony as its official agents and representing the uncompromising Puritan wing, hindered rather than helped the cause by insisting that no concessions should be made and that Massachusetts should receive a confirmation of all her former privileges. Mather's success was noteworthy. He could not prevent the appointment of a royal governor or the separation of

New Hampshire from Massachusetts, nor could he obtain the right of coinage for the colony; but he did secure the permanent annexation of Maine and the Plymouth colony, and a large measure of appointive power and legislative control for the people. In some ways most significant of all, he obtained from the Crown the noteworthy concession that the council of the colony should be chosen by the general assembly and not be appointed from England, as was the case with all the other royal colonies. Even New Hampshire eventually had the same governor as Massachusetts, thus preserving a union for all central and northern New England, which was destined to last for forty-four years.

The charter of 1691 was a compromise between the old government which had existed in Massachusetts since 1630 and that of a regular royal colony, and as such it satisfied neither party. It was greeted in Massachusetts with vehement disapproval by the old faction, who charged Mather with flagrantly deserting his trust; and in England it was viewed as a shameful concession to the whims of the Puritans. This yoking together of parts of two systems, corporate and royal, was to give rise in Massachusetts in the succeeding century to a struggle for control that deeply affected the course of the colony's later history.

In all the New England colonies, the fall of Andros and the close of the century marked the end of an era in which the dominant impulse was the religious purpose that actuated the original colonists in coming to America. The desire for a political isolation that would preserve the established religious system intact was exceedingly strong in the seventeenth century, but it ceased to be as strong in the century that followed. The fathers gave way to the children; the settlements grew rapidly in size, increased their output of staple products beyond what they needed for themselves, and became vastly interested in trade and commerce with all parts of the Atlantic world. Towns grew into larger towns and cities; and Portsmouth, Newbury, Salem, Marblehead, Boston, Newport, New London, Hartford, Wethersfield, Middletown, New Haven, Fairfield, and Stamford became, in varying degrees, centers of an increasing population and of new business interests that brought New England into closer contact with the other colonies, with the West Indies, and with the Old

World. England became involved in the long struggle with France and not only called on the colonies to aid her in military campaigns against the French in America, but endeavored to bring them within the scope of her colonial empire. All these influences tended to expand the life of New England and to force its people more and more out of their isolation. Yet, despite this fact, the Puritan colonies — Connecticut and Rhode Island especially — continued to lie in large part outside the pale of British control and example, and their inhabitants continued to accept religion and the Puritan standards of morals as the guide of their daily lives.

BIBLIOGRAPHICAL NOTE

THE standard authority on the subjects treated in the volume is J. G. Palfrey, *History of New England*, 5 vols. (1858–1864, 1875–1890), a work of broad scholarship and written in a not uninteresting style, but indiscriminating in its defense of Massachusetts and without any understanding of the purpose and attitude of the English authorities. In somewhat the same class are G. E. Ellis, *The Puritan Age* (1888), a dry book but less given to special pleading, and Justin Winsor, *The Memorial History of Boston*, 4 vols. (1880–1882), a series of essays with elaborate notes and bibliographies, presenting in a fragmentary way the conventional view of the period. Less frankly favorable to New England is J. A. Doyle, *English Colonies in America: The Puritan Colonies*, 2 vols. (1887), a work of value, but diffuse in style and often confused in treatment, and, though written by an Englishman, displaying little interest in the English side of the story. The chapters in Edward Channing, *History of the United States*, vol. i (1905), that relate to the subject, are scholarly and always interesting; while those in H. L. Osgood, *The American Colonies in the Seventeenth Century*, 3 vols. (1904–1907), contain the ablest accounts we have of the institutional characteristics of the period.

There are few good histories of the individual colonies. Those deserving of mention are: Thomas Hutchinson, *History of Massachusetts Bay*, 2 vols. (1764–1767); S. G. Arnold, *History of the State of Rhode Island*, 2 vols. (4th ed. 1894); Irving B. Richman, *Rhode Island* (1904, American Commonwealth Series); B. Trumbull, *Complete History of Connecticut*, 2 vols. (new ed. 1898); A. Johnson, *Connecticut* (2d ed. 1903, American Commonwealth Series); E. Atwater, *History of the Colony of New Haven* (1881); W. H. Fry, *New Hampshire as a Royal Province* (1908); W. D. Williamson, *History of the State of Maine* (1832); H. S. Burrage, *The Beginnings of Colonial Maine* (1914). Hutchinson and Trumbull are classics; Arnold is one of the best of the state histories; Richman and Johnson are short and readable; Fry deals with the institutional life of the colony; Williamson is old-fashioned and poor; but Burrage is authoritative.

Special works are: H. M. Dexter, *The England and Holland of the Pilgrims* (1905), a very valuable and learned account; C. F. Adams, *Three Episodes of Massachusetts History*, 2 vols. (1892), treating of the antecedents of Boston, the Antinomian Controversy, and church and town government, the first essay especially being indispensable; R. M. Jones, *The Quakers in the American Colonies* (1911), the fairest account of the Quakers in New England. W. De L. Love, *The Colonial History of Hartford* (1914); W. E. Weeden, *Early Rhode Island* (1910); and G. S. Kimball, *Providence in Colonial Times* (1912), are in every way excellent, that of Love being a minutely critical analysis of the Connecticut settlement. W. E. Weeden, *Social and Economic History of New England*, 2 vols. (1891), is a valuable collection of information. Certain chapters in Edward Eggleston's *Transit of Civilization* (1901) treat of the mental outfit of the colonists; and M. W. Jernegan in the *School Review*, June, 1915, deals with the beginnings of public education in New England; G. L. Beer, *Origins of the British Colonial System*, 1660–1688, 2 vols. (1912), and C. M. Andrews, *British Committees, Commissions, and Councils of Trade and Plantations, 1622–1675* (1908), concern British policy and administration in the seventeenth century.

Biographies varying greatly in value and manner of treatment follow: R. C. Winthrop, *Life and Letters of John Winthrop*, 2 vols. (2d ed. 1869); G. L. Walker. *Thomas Hooker* (1891, Makers of America Series); J. H. Twichell, *John Winthrop* (1891, *id.*); A. Steele, *Elder Brewster* (1857); L. G. Jones, *Samuel Gorton* (1896); A. Gorton, *The Life and Times of Samuel Gorton* (1907); O. S. Straus, *Roger Williams* (1894); M. E. Hall, *Roger Williams* (1917); T. W. Bicknell, *Story of Dr. John Clarke* (1915); J. M. Taylor, *Roger Ludlow* (1900); J. K. Hosmer, *Young Sir Harry Vane* (1888); *A Memoir of Sir John Leverett, Knt.* (1856); and in *American Biography*, 10 vols., are lives of John Mason by G. E. Ellis, Roger Williams by William Gammell, Samuel Gorton by John M. Mackie, and Anne Hutchinson by G. E. Ellis, though none of them is particularly satisfactory.

The original sources for the period are: the *Acts of the Privy Council, Colonial*, vols. i, ii (1908–1910); *The Calendar of State Papers, Colonial*, vols. i–viii, 1574–1692 (1860–1901); and the colonial records of Plymouth, Massachusetts Bay, Connecticut, Rhode Island, and New Hampshire. Collections of narratives and letters may be found in the publications of the Prince Society [C. H. Bell, *John Wheelwright and his Writings* (1876); C. F. Adams, *Morton's New England Canaán* (1883); C. W. Tuttle, *Capt. John Mason* (1887); J. P. Baxter, *Sir Ferdinando Gorges*, 3 vols. (1890); C. F. Adams, *Antinomianism in the Colony of Massachusetts Bay* (1894); R. N. Toppan, *Edward Randolph*, 7 vols. (1898–1909, last two volumes edited by A. T. S. Goodrick)]; and in the *Original Narratives of Early American History* [W. T. Davis, *Bradford's History of Plymouth Plantation* (1908); J. K. Hosmer, *Winthrop's Journal*, 2 vols. (1908); J. F. Jameson, *Johnson's Wonder-Working Providence of Sion's Saviour in New England* (1911); C. H. Lincoln, *Narratives of the Indian Wars* (1913); G. L. Burr, *Narratives of the Witchcraft Cases* (1914); C. M. Andrews, *Narratives of the Insurrections* (1915)]. A sumptuous edition of Bradford's history has been edited for the Massachusetts Historical Society, by W. C. Ford, 2 vols. (1915). S. Sewall's *Diary*, 3 vols. (Mass. Hist. Soc. *Coll.*, 5th series, 1878–1882) and Cotton Mather's *Magnalia*, 2 vols. (1853) are important. W. Walker, *The Creeds and Platforms of Congregationalism* (1893) is of great value. C. W. Sawyer, *Firearms in American History* (1910), has an excellent chapter on firearms in colonial times.

The articles on *Boston, New England, Massachusetts, Plymouth, Friends* (*Society of*), etc., in *The Encyclopædia Britannica*, 11th Edition, should be referred to for additional bibliographies.

INDEX

Agawam (Springfield), 61, 62

Allerton, Isaac, 17

Ambrose, The, ship, 29

Amsterdam, Separatists gather at, 7

"Ancient and Honorable Artillery," 135

Andros, Sir Edmund, takes part in case against Massachusetts, 156; Governor of Massachusetts, 174 *et seq.*; strengthens fortifications, 179–80; New York and New Jersey added to his domain, 183–84; attention confined to Massachusetts, 184–85; recalled, 196

Anne, The, ship, 13

Aquidneck, Island of, 48, 55

Arbella, The, ship, 29

Aspinwall, 48

Augsburg, settlement of (1555), 4

Aulnay-Charnisé, Charles de Menou, Sieur d', 95–96

Bartlett, Robert, 84

Bay Colony, *see* Massachusetts Bay Colony

Blackstone, William, 23, 24

Blessing of the Bay, The, ship, 78

Boston, Puritans from England settle at, 29; half the colonists live in or near, 35; treatment of Quakers in, 79–80; importance of, 164; grows into a city, 198; *see also* Shawmut

Boswell, Sir William, quoted, 97

Bradford, William, in Scrooby, 7; quoted, 15–16; Governor of Plymouth, 17; *History of Plimouth Plantation*, 19; dead before 1660, 78

Bradstreet, Governor of Massachusetts, 191

Bradstreet, Simon, 103

Branford, (Conn.), 70

Brenten, Governor, quoted, 114

Brewster, William, father of William, elder of Plymouth, 6

Brewster, William, Elder of Plymouth, 6, 8

Browne, John, 41

Browne, Samuel, 41

Bulkeley, Peter, 156

Cambridge platform (1648), 79

Canonchet, Indian chief, 142, 143, 144

Carr, Sir Robert, 119, 122

Cartwright, George, Colonel, 119, 122

Carver, John, Governor of Plymouth, 13

Charity, The, ship, 13

Charlestown (Mass.), 29, 35

Charter Oak, 181

Child, Dr. Robert, 38, 116

Church, Benjamin, Captain, 142

Clarendon, Lord, Prime Minister of England, 113, 116, 117, 120–21, 126

Clark, John, of Newbury, 83

Clarke, Dr. John, 47, 48, 103, 106, 112, 113

Clayton, Richard, 6

Coddington, William, 43, 47, 48, 49, 54–55

Coggeshall, one of founders of Portsmouth, 48

Connecticut, leaders who influenced, 47; settled by Massachusetts people, 56; four claimants for, 57; migration from Massachusetts, 57–61; commission government, 60–61; government, 62–64; witchcraft in, 81; sends petition to England, 103–04; charter granted (1662), 108; extends authority of colony, 108–10; claims Long Island, 130; title under charter recognized by Massachusetts, 131; debates joining New York, 173; Andros endeavors to bring under control, 180; consents to join Massachusetts, 180–82; renews old forms, 192

Cooke, a leader of conservatives in Boston, 164

Cotton, John, 78

Council for Foreign Plantations, Committee of the, 34

Danforth, a leader of conservatives in Boston, 164

Davenport, John, of New Haven, 47, 67, 68, 78, 111, 112

Deerfield (Mass.), massacre of, 141

Delfthaven, Pilgrims embark at, 10

Denonville, Marquis de, Governor of Canada, 178

Denton, Richard, 70

Desborough, 78

Dongan, Colonel, Governor of New York, 178, 180, 183

Dorchester (Mass.), 35

Dover (N. H.), 65, 66

Downing, Emanuel, 35

Dudley, Joseph, 168, 169–70, 173–74

Dudley, Thomas, 28

Dyer, Mary, 80

Eaton, Samuel, 67

Eaton, Theophilus, 47, 67, 68, 69

Education in New England, 83–85

Eliot, John, 94

Endecott, John, in congregation of Rev. John White, 24; sent as governor to Salem, 25; disregards claims of Gorges, 26; defaces royal ensign at Salem, 32; banishes colonists for religious differences, 41; signs petition to England, 104

England, in early seventeenth century, 2 et seq.; awakes to importance of colonies, 101–102; new colonial policy, 102–103; affairs in seventeenth century, 126–27; attitude toward Massachusetts, 150; finances under Charles II., 151–152; future of New England decided in, 194

Exeter (N. H.), 65, 66

Fairfield (Conn.), 198

Feudal system in England, 2, 3

Fortune, The, ship, 13

Fuller, Dr. Samuel, 37, 83

Fundamental orders, 62–64

Gardiner, Sir Christopher, 31, 41

George, Captain of the Rose, 190

Gilds, 3–4

Goodyear, Stephen, 77

Gorges, Sir Ferdinando, 22–23, 25, 26, 29–30, 30–34, 65

Gorges, Robert, 23, 25

Gorges, Thomas, 35

Gorton, Samuel, 49–51

Graham, Attorney-General of Massachusetts, 187, 191

"Great Fundamentals, The," 18

Greenwich (Conn.), 109, 133

Guilford (Conn.), 70, 109

Half-Way Covenant, 79, 93–94
Hampton (N. H.), 66
Handmaid, The, ship, 13
Hartford (Conn.), 61, 198
Harvard College, 84, 93
Hawkins, Jane, 83
Haynes, John, 35, 47, 58, 78
Higginson, Francis, 37
Hilton, Edward, 65
Holmes, O. W., quoted, 83
Holmes, William, 56
Hooke, 78
Hooker, Thomas, 47, 58, 60, 61, 62, 78
Hopkins, Edward, Governor, 84
House of Good Hope, 56
Humphrey, John, 28
Hutchinson, Anne, 41–42, 48, 98

Indians, trouble with, 133 *et seq.*; dealings with, 138–39; number in New England, 139

Jewel, The, ship, 29
Johnson, Lady Arabella, 35
Johnson, Isaac, 28
Jones, Christopher, captain of the *Mayflower*, 11–12

King Philip's War (1675–76), 136, 138, 139, 140–46
Kingfisher, The, ship, 174
Kirke, Percy, Colonel, 166–67

Lathrop, John, 67
La Tour, Charles de, 95–96
Laud, Archbishop, 32
Laud Commission, 34
Leete, Governor, 111
Leyden, Separatists move to, 7
London, as a center of Separatism, 6
Long Island, uncertainty as to jurisdiction, 129–30
Ludlow, Roger, 47, 58, 78, 98
Lynn, Henry, 41

Maine, settled, 65; under jurisdiction of Massachusetts, 66–67; status undecided, 132; military preparedness, 135; permanently annexed to Massachusetts, 197
Marblehead (Mass.), 198
Mason, John, Captain, 30–31, 34, 65, 136
Massachusetts Bay Colony, 21 *et seq.*; begins as fishing venture, 24; obtains patent for land, 25; founded, 29; Gorges attempts overthrow of, 30–34; growth (1630–40), 34–36; time of stress, 36; government, 37–40; religious intolerance, 41–43; commercial ventures, 78; leader among colonies, 100–01; sends petition to King, 103; restoration of Stuarts causes trouble for, 104–05; charter confirmed, 105; religious liberty defined by King, 105–06; inquiry into affairs by Clarendon, 116–18; commissioners sent to, 118 *et seq.*; franchise law modified, 121; defies commission, 123–126; recognizes Connecticut's title (1672), 131; asserts right to control Maine and New Hampshire, 132; military preparedness, 135; Randolph inquires into affairs, 147; new instructions to royal governors, 148–49; attitude of England toward, 148–52; inquiry by Randolph, 154–56; mission sent to England, 156–57; purchases title to Maine and estranges England further, 158–59; royal orders in regard to trade and religious liberty, 159–60; attitude toward England, 160–61; sends agents to England, 162; charter forfeited (1684), 163; grows more liberal, 164; territory enlarged, 166; a royal colony, 166 *et seq.*; preliminary royal

Massachusetts Bay Colony—*Con.*
government, 168–69; changes
in life of people, 170–73;
faults in royal government,
185–89; government of An-
dros overthrown, 190; resumes
self-government, 191; sends
Mather to England, 194–96;
charter of 1691, 197

Massachusetts Bay Company,
charter gr·nted (1629), 26;
control passes to Puritans, 27

Massachusetts Commission, per-
sonnel, 118–19; object, 120–
121; failure, 123–26

Mather, Cotton, quoted, 79

Mather, Increase, 194–95, 196

Maverick, Samuel, 23, 38, 116
et seq.

Mayflower, The, ship, 10, 11

Mayflower Compact, 12–13

Merrymount, 22

Middletown (Conn.), 198

Milford (Conn.), 70

Mishawum (Charlestown), 24

Moody, Lady Deborah, 35

Morrell, 23

Morton, Thomas, 22, 31, 34, 41,
47

Mount Wollaston, 22

Mystic, taken into Connecticut,
109

Naumkeag (Salem), 25

New Amsterdam, seized by
English, 110

New England, people of, 72–73;
settled by radicals, 73–74; lack
of toleration in, 74; town life,
75–76; local color in various
settlements, 76–78; witchcraft, 80–81; superstitions of
people, 81–82; medicine and
surgery, 82–83; education, 83–
85; travel, 85–86; homes, 86;
money, 86–87; reckoning of
time, 87; respect for grants
and charters, 88; attitude
toward England, 88–90; organization in, 89; rivalry with
Dutch and French, 90–91;
confederation of colonies, 91
et seq.; trouble with the French,
94–96; trouble with the Dutch,
96–98; period of readjustment,
129 *et seq.*; Indian troubles,
133 *et seq.*; boundary disputes,
133; population, 139; menace
from French, 177–79; Dominion of, 182–83; brought closer
to English control, 199

New England Canaan, Morton,
32

New England Confederation *see*
United Colonies of New
England

New England Council, 9, 12,
22, 26, 30, 32–33

New Hampshire, influential
leaders in, 47; controversy
over title, 65; under jurisdiction of Massachusetts, 66–67;
separation from Massachu-
setts, 67, 71; status un-
decided, 132; military preparedness, 135

New Haven, influential leaders
in, 47; settled, 67–68; government, 68–70; combines other
plantations under her, 70–71;
absorbed by Conn., 71; commercial ventures, 77–78; witchcraft in, 81; misfortunes of,
110–11; surrenders to Connecticut, 111–12; confederation
dissolved, 112

New London (Conn.), 198

New Netherlands, conquest of,
122

New Somersetshire, 65

Newark, founded, 112

Newbury, 198

Newport (R. I.), 49, 198

Nicholson, Francis, 183

Nicolls, Richard, 118, 119, 122

Norfolk, a center of Separatism,
6

Norton, John, 103

Nowell, a leader of conservatives in Boston, 164

Oldham, John, 56

Palmer, Judge, 187, 191
Partridge, Captain, 54, 55
Pawcatuck, taken into Connecticut, 109
Pequot War (1637), 136-37
Peters, Hugh, 59, 78
Pierson, Abraham, 46, 47, 112
Pilgrims, leave for Holland (1607-08), 7; reasons for leaving Holland, 8; decide to go to America, 8-9; conditions under which expedition was undertaken, 10; journey of the *Mayflower*, 10-12; draw up covenant, 12; life in Plymouth Colony, 14-19; greatness lies in religious influence, 19-20
Plymouth Colony, founded, 12-20; secures right to establish fishing colony, 24; submits to authority of Massachusetts, 71; fishing and trading, 77; witchcraft in, 81; sends mission to England, 104; military preparedness, 135; renews old forms, 192; permanently annexed to Massachusetts, 197
Plymouth, town of, 18
Pocasset (Portsmouth), 48
Portsmouth (N. H.), 66, 198
Portsmouth (R. I.), 51-52; *see also* Pocasset
Protestantism, controlled by state, 4
Providence, settled, 47-48; court of arbitration at, 51; charter unites with other settlements, 53; government under patent, 53-54
Puritans, obtain control of Massachusetts Bay Company, 27; reach Salem (1630), 29; become Separatists, 37; characteristics of the frontier, 46-47
Pynchon, William, 60, 62, 77

Quakers, come to Boston (1656), 79; treatment, 79-80
Quinnipiac, 68

Randolph, Edward, 147, 152-156, 160, 161, 162, 163, 167, 168, 173, 174, 196
Ratcliffe, Philip, 31, 41
Ratcliffe, Robert, 168-69, 171, 173
Reformation, The, 3
Rhode Island, leaders in, 47; individualism in, 56; colony of separatism, 79; not included in Confederation of colonies, 92; applies for charter, 103; conflicting boundary claims, 113; charter granted, (1663), 113-14; rival claims to, 115; unsettled conditions, 131; surrenders charter, 173; sends council members to Boston, 180; renews old forms, 192
Rhode Island settlements, Providence, 47-48; Pocasset, 48-49; Newport, 49; Shawomet or Warwick, 49
Robinson, John, 6-7, 8
Rossiter, Bray, of Guilford, 83, 111
Rowlandson, Mrs., 143
Roxbury (Mass.), 35

Salem (Mass.), 25, 198; *see also* Naumkeag
Salem witchcraft, 81
Saltonstall, Sir Richard, 28, 35
Saybrook, 33, 40
Saye and Sele, Lord, 33, 106-07
Scott, John, Captain, 109, 130
Scrooby, Nottinghamshire, a center of Separatism, 6
Separatists, 5 *et seq.*
Setauket, 130

Shawmut (Boston), 23
Shawomet, 49
Sheffield, Lord, 24
Slavery forbidden in Rhode Island (1652), 54
Smith, John, 3, 11
Southold on Long Island, 70, 109
Speedwell, The, ship, 10
Springfield (Mass.), becomes part of Mass., 62; center of fur trade, 77; *see also* Agawam
Stamford (Conn.), 70, 109, 133, 198
Standish, Miles, 3
Stiles party, 57
Stone, Samuel, 60
Stoughton, William, 156
Stuyvesant, Peter, 97, 109

Talbot, The, ship, 29

Uncas, Indian chief, 137
Underhill, 47
United Colonies of New England, 91

Vane, Henry, 33, 35, 40, 59
Vassall, William, 38
Virginia Company of London, 9
Virginia Company of Plymouth, 9

Walford, 24, 41
Warwick, Earl of, 25, 26, 28, 30, 32
Warwick, a Rhode Island settlement, 49

Watertown (Mass.), 35
Wessagusset (Quincy), 21, 22, 23
West, Secretary of Mass., 187, 191
Weston, Thomas, 10, 21
Wethersfield (Conn.), 61, 198
Weymouth (Mass.), 23
Wheelwright, John, 47, 65
White, Rev. John, 24, 27
Whitfield, 78
Whiting, 78
Williams, Roger, driven from Boston, 47; locates at Providence, 47-48; obtains charter, 52-53; quoted, 54; goes to England to confirm patent, 55; in 1660, 78
Windsor (Conn.), 61
Winnissimmet (Chelsea), 23-24
Winslow, Edward, 17, 38, 50, 52
Winslow, John, 190
Winslow, Josiah, General, 142
Winthrop, John, elected Governor of Mass. Bay Colony, 28; leader among the Puritans, 35; died before 1660, 78
Winthrop, John, son of the Governor, 40, 59, 83, 103-04, 106-07
Wise, John, 186
Witchcraft in New England, 80-81
Wollaston, Captain, 22
Wright, Richard, 41

Young, Alse, 81
Young, Captain, 130